More Than Just A Pretty Face

by Victoria Best

WARNING This book contains graphic crime scene details and statements that some may find very disturbing.

"This is a work of nonfiction. No names have been changed, no characters invented, no events fabricated."

More Than Just A Pretty Face

by Victoria Best

Published by

RJ Parker Publishing

All Rights Reserved

April 2019

ISBN 13: 978-1987902594
ISBN 10:1987902599

Editing and Cover Design by
Evening Sky Publishing Services

Published in Canada

Copyrights

Table of Contents

Prologue

Many have asked me about my interest in Rodney Alcala and why I chose to write about him. To answer that question, it wasn't actually a choice I made. As fate would have it, the decision was made for me.

In March 2010, I was watching the news of the day on TV. A program was airing about a serial killer, showing photos he had taken decades before. This particular serial killer had been in prison since 1980, but his photos were never released to the public. Law enforcement was obligated to defer publishing them until all trials, appeals, and court proceedings had run its due process. Astonishingly, it took until 2010 for this to conclude. Back when the serial killer was arrested, the photos were found locked away in a secret storage locker, along with jewelry taken from his victims. I was fascinated to see that now, after all this time, the photos were being released in hopes that someone would recognize them.

Despite there being nearly 2000 photos, only a fraction of them could be released because of their graphic nature. Hundreds of nudes, many of a sexually explicit nature, were among them. The photos released showed a variety of situations. Mostly smiling girls, but you could tell the photographs were cropped tightly so the nudity was hidden. Some girls were clearly flirting with the camera and having fun. But there were also some girls who were clearly troubled, with fear in their eyes. It was impossible not to wonder if they were told they were going to be murdered before the photo was taken, or if some of these photos were taken after they had been assaulted? It is even possible that all of the photos were of those who later became his victim. I was told there were photographs showing victims in various states of consciousness, and even some where the girls looked dead, or heavily drugged.

One of the more explicit photos was released with the rest in error. It included a young person, appearing to do a backbend, eyes half closed, and hair strewn about. The position was an unnatural one. Since the photo was cropped, it was hard to tell if the subject was male or female. And the sex of the youth was widely debated on crime forums. The person was draped over a tree branch. They were wearing jeans that appeared to be wet. Their hair was below the shoulders in length, and reddish-brown in color. To me, the person did not appear to be alive. We know that Alcala enjoyed posing his victims after death. That particular photo will not be included here; however, I look at it every day to motivate me to complete this book.

That day in 2010, when I was looking at the photos, I wondered what kind of monster would hurt these innocent and jubilant-looking young people. Some could have been taken from a day in the life of Greenwich Village, instead of the last photo taken by a serial killer. Who was the person who took these photos? And did he look like your neighbor next door, as these guys often do?

As Rodney Alcala's face was broadcast onto the television screen, I suddenly felt a roar in my ears as if I was going to pass out. I felt a wave of nausea as the impossible started to permeate into my brain. I sat down, and didn't hear much else in the news broadcast as my mind raced through the past, to a time decades before, when the realization came to me – I personally knew this serial killer.

****

With the blackest of hair and pale green eyes that reminded me of pistachio nuts, my mother was my hero. People would turn to watch her enter a room. She didn't seem to mind at all being the center of attention. That's just the way it was. In elementary school, I thought I had the prettiest mother, and I was the luckiest little girl. She always wore the prettiest dresses to accent her eyes and hair, and I loved her so much. Often, in our travels, people would mistake her for a film and stage actress, Gene Tierney. Tierney was known as one of the most beautiful women in film, and I was proud that my mother resembled her. I wondered if that was the reason she received so many second glances. I liked to think it was just her own beauty people were seeing.

Mom was my best friend, and she rarely went anywhere fun without me. We shopped together, we sunbathed by the pool together, and we gossiped like girlfriends. Even though she had her own friends and was quite popular, I was an only child, and received all of her attention. She often preferred spending time with me instead of women her own age. Then, when my sister was born in April of 1966, things changed. But, during the early to mid-sixties, I definitely enjoyed the life of a spoiled child.

One morning, in the fall of 1965, Mom woke me up early with the surprise news we were going to San Francisco for the day to shop for new clothes. We lived in a small town of about 6,500 people, so our shopping was quite limited. San Francisco, only 2 hours away, was almost always our place to go. Nowadays, it's not acceptable to call a woman a 'clothes horse,' but back in the day, my mom owned that title. In my house, you could always see a colorful shopping bag, or three, sitting on a table, on mom's bed, in the corners of her bedroom, or the back of her closet. Today, I still blame my outlandish storage and container obsession on her for all of the lovely bags and boxes she would keep shiny new toys in. That was not the only way I connected with my mother, and how she impacted my life though. I knew exactly what it meant when mom said we were going shopping for clothes. I devoured my breakfast in short order to get an early start.

After breakfast, I jumped in her convertible to head for Fisherman's Wharf in San Francisco. Our routine was to go to the Wharf first, eat fish and chips, and then head over to Macy's, where we would shop until we were both beat. We parked near the wharf, and I rolled my car window down, taking in a big breath of sea air. I was hungry again, and anxious to start shopping. My mouth watered, as I smelled the aroma of fried fish mingling with the ocean breeze.

I noticed 'him' before any other person in the seating area of the outdoor restaurant. He stood out like a Ken doll in a pile of Barbies. He didn't seem to notice me as I walked past him on my way to the restroom. My mother was sitting at our little table, enjoying her soda. He was looking at my mom. There was no doubt about it. Leaning against a fence post, his sooty eyes and brooding good looks made me wonder if he might be someone famous, perhaps even a movie star. It wasn't unlikely to see celebrities in San Francisco in the sixties. I walked right in front of him. I could have even tripped over him, but I don't think he would have noticed me. His eyes were trained on her like an animal's on its prey. It was disorienting to feel the deep intensity of his eyes going through me as they bore down on my mother. He had an intensity that I'd never encountered before. Although I was too young to fully grasp what I was witnessing, it was the first time I remember being envious of someone being attentive of her first. I wasn't surprised at this man staring at her since I was used to people admiring her.

When I walked back towards our table after using the restroom, I forced myself not to look in his direction. I didn't even know if he was still there. Even if I was making too much of it, I decided to tell her about the young, handsome man who seemed to be so enthralled with her. At the table, I lowered my head, leaned in towards her, and began to whisper in her ear about what I had noticed a few minutes before. She instinctively looked in his direction, much to my discomfort. I tried not to, but I couldn't help glancing in his direction as well, and noticed he was still there. But now, he had moved to get a better view of our table. He flashed a shy grin as my mom turned to look directly at him. I felt my face turning warm with embarrassment as I realized both my mom and I were now both staring at him.

He strolled towards our table in what seemed like slow motion. I cursed myself for telling, as much as an innocent girl could, and knew the freckles across my nose and cheeks were turning an ugly and splotchy crimson. I knew at that moment, I looked absolutely ridiculous. However, he didn't even seem to notice me. He seemed beguiled with the impressive woman sitting next to me, my mom. I half expected him to fall to one knee at any moment, and kiss the hand of this glorious woman.

Instead, he hesitated, stopping in his tracks. For the first time, he seemed to see me sitting with her. The intensity of his gaze was the same, but now it was fixed on me. He pulled up a chair and sat down. I was in awe of how much nerve it would take to just walk up to a stranger and sit down at their table without asking permission. Yet, he did it with ease. Like he had done it a million times. As I sat there with my red, freckled face, feeling completely foolish, and my eyes looking down at the table, he introduced himself as Rod Alcala. He chatted and joked with my mom, but he never left me out of the conversation. He seemed to always bring the discussion back to me. So I didn't feel left out, I suppose. I appreciated him doing this. He asked how old I was, what grade I was in, and what school I attended.

Looking back, I was very impressionable. He was a man in his early twenties, but I saw myself as a teenager, and was utterly dazzled by him. My mother was 38-years-old, but she looked much younger. Maybe he thought that she might be a good match for him at first, only to discover after sitting down that she was a wife, and a mother. When we all went on our way that day, plans were made for Rod to visit us at our home. And I was thrilled.

My father traveled a lot for work and was usually away during the week, and home only on weekends. He had little to say about how mom and I spent our time. She seemed to be the one to make the house rules. We had the biggest and best television that money could buy, and a swimming pool in our back yard. Given the heat of the California days, a pool was a necessity. We swam before and after school during the week when school was in session, and from dawn to dusk in the summer. My friends were often there and my house seemed to be the neighborhood teen hangout.

I don't recall the circumstances of him visiting, or even how many times he did. I do remember one time though that his visit did not seem to go well. He arrived, and was only there for perhaps 15 minutes. He seemed nervous, angry, or somewhat out of sorts. He revved his motorcycle in our driveway before he came inside and he seemed considerably different than I'd ever seen him before. I remember thinking that it was odd that he'd be leaving so soon after the long drive to get to our place. Thinking back now, it's possible he had a disagreement with my mother. I can't say why or even if that was the case. I just remember the incident as being very odd. Perhaps he wanted my mother to do something with him, or maybe he had asked to take me for a ride on his motorcycle, and my mom said no. I remember wanting to ride on that motorcycle so much. I had asked her once but her answer was no. Knowing what I do now, maybe he planned to do something that day, and it made him angry that his plans were ruined.

My next memory of him was a remote one, an echo in the dark recesses of my mind. For years, whenever I would recall it, I was convinced it wasn't as big a deal as I'd made it out to be. Only after I found out who he really was, and what he was capable of, that I broke out in a cold sweat imagining what might have happened.

It was in the spring of 1966, when I had one of the most frightening episodes of my life. Although, I didn't realize until decades later what made it such a terrifying experience. I always had an active imagination, and enjoyed telling scary stories with my friends about vampires, werewolves, and the horrible monster/man with a claw for a hand that haunted all parking teenagers. But what could have happened to me was real, and on a whole different level of scary.

One night in our pool, I was floating on my back, looking up at the stars, enjoying the clear, cool water. Our pool was painted turquoise about three-quarters of the way up from the bottom. I loved swimming at night with only the blue glow of the pool lights on. The night air in California was always perfect for night-time swimming, and several times a week I would swim alone. As perfect as it was, I wasn't supposed to do it. And I knew it. Still, it was one of the rules my parents gave me that I broke.

Bouncing my way from the steps to the deep end, I forced my body down to the bottom of the pool, and propelled myself back up out of the water.

I loved to twirl like a dancer, and see how high I could launch myself from the bottom. That night, I had just propelled myself up out of the water, when I thought I saw movement by the corner of our fence. I dismissed it, but remember spending a little more time under the water surface as I sat on the bottom of the pool. I figured my mind was playing tricks on me. I was too scared to surface and face what was there, but the burning in my lungs told me I had to.

It was perhaps eight feet from where I was to the corner of the fence where I saw movement. I propelled myself up again, but this time I didn't turn like a dancer as I broke the surface of the water. I faced the corner of the fence instead. Forcing my eyelids to open through the sting of the chlorine, they widened in panic as I saw the outline of a man. I knew immediately that it was Rod Alcala. He was standing there, on the outside of our fence, watching me. His long hair, and the frame of his face was visible, yet the shadows and darkness masked his features. I will never know why, but something within me registered danger. I froze in fear for a brief second. Somehow, I found the courage to turn my body, and literally ran through the water, half flapping my arms and half swimming. I slammed my right ankle into the second stair of the pool, unable to process the pain as I scraped it. I fell up the stairs, praying that I could make it across the patio and into the house safely. I did, but I was shivering as I slammed the patio door shut, locking it behind me. My parents were asleep so I made as little sound as possible as I ran to every door in the house and locked them too. Back in those days, we never locked our doors. I was afraid to wake up my parents and tell them because I was didn't want to get in trouble. I remember shaking in fear all night long. I tried to convince myself that what I saw was just my imagination. But I will never forget hearing the rumble of a motorcycle starting up, and I know to this day that it was 'him' there that night.

Chapter 1: Serial Killers

"On a dark desert highway
Cool wind in my hair
Warm smell of colitas
Rising up through the air
Up ahead in the distance
I saw a shimmering light
My head grew heavy and my sight grew dim
I had to stop for the night
There she stood in the doorway
I heard the mission bell
And I was thinking to myself
This could be Heaven or this could be Hell"
Then she lit up a candle
And she showed me the way
There were voices down the corridor
I thought I heard them say
Welcome to the Hotel California
Such a lovely place (Such a lovely place)
Such a lovely face
Plenty of room at the Hotel California
Any time of year (Any time of year)
You can find it here"

− "Hotel California" by The Eagles

They roam like animals, stalking their prey, their minds deplete of any human trait like compassion, shame, or self-control. Whether they follow a victim for weeks, or see someone suddenly and it just hits them, they are always ready to strike in the blink of an eye. When they attack, they are almost always successful. Most victims don't even have a chance to scream. They perfect their onslaught with stealth and strategy. Many of them are 'sit and wait' killers, and in the 1960s through to the 1980s when they were most prevalent, they seemed to be everywhere. They are serial killers.

It seems ironic that the Smiley Face symbol found on everything in the mid-sixties, was a gruesome reminder of the evil that was about to take over the United States in the next decade. In the 1970s, the U.S. experienced an alarming surge in the number of active serial killers. Radford University Serial Killer Information Center reports that during that decade, 450 serial killers were active at any given moment in America...a substantially higher number than the 156 serial killers reported for the previous decade.

What caused the outbreak of this type of killer? Were there so many more brutal and unbalanced human hunters wandering America, or did law enforcement agencies simply become better equipped to identify and catch them?

While the social atmosphere of the sixties helped spread messages of peace and free love in America, the seventies brought an atmosphere of dread and fear. News about a new serial killer traumatizing American cities seemed to pop up every month.

Charles Manson and his 'family' became the poster children of such shocking murders. Manson directed his cult to kill Sharon Tate, her unborn child, Leno and Rosemary LaBianca, and four others in 1969. They were found guilty of the murders on January 25, 1971. The killers were originally sentenced to death. Later, California abolished the Death Penalty, which automatically changed their sentences to life in prison.

While it's true the Manson Family murders sent a shockwave through America like no other, in reality, at the same time those murders occurred, another type of killer, equally terrifying, was tormenting the San Francisco Bay area.

The *Zodiac Killer* introduced a new age of serial killer...one bold and intelligent enough to get away with their crimes, but also one who craved notoriety, and demanded credit for what they did. Zodiac mailed a series of cryptograms and coded letters to the press. In the letters, Zodiac admitted to several murders, and threatened to kill again. He is believed to be responsible for killing at least five people during the late sixties, maybe more. He was never caught. While law enforcement investigated several suspects, no one has ever been conclusively identified, let alone convicted, of being the *Zodiac Killer*.

Serial Killers like Ted Bundy, John Wayne Gacy, Dennis Rader, and Rodney Alcala were men who lived up to the title of serial killer with their savage hearts. The nature of their cold-blooded murders unleashed a whole new kind of terror on the cities where they hunted. The severity and brutality with which they took human life shocked even the most seasoned law enforcement officers.

Although not as well known as Bundy, Gacy, or Rader, Alcala was argued by some to be the most prolific killer of them all. Given the ease with which he mobilized across the entire country, his access to potential victims was infinite. And there were many gaps in his timeline where his whereabouts were unknown. It's impossible to know the true number of his victims.

Serial Killer Ted Bundy described himself as "the most cold-hearted son of a bitch you'll ever meet." His sickening crimes were proof to that statement. Yet, he was an attractive, likable, and outgoing man who was attending law school and working on political campaigns. He was a skilled manipulator who was able to lure more than 36 women to their deaths.

Bundy showed an intense interest in 'all things gruesome' at an early age. In his childhood, he became enamored with knives. He was a timid but smart child. He did well in school, but did not play well with others. When he was a teenager, the darker side of Bundy's character started to really develop. He enjoyed 'peeping tom' type activities, peeking into other people's windows, and breaking in to steal anything he wanted.

There is disagreement on exactly when Bundy started killing, and there is not one single victim said to be his first. But around 1974, women started going missing from the Pacific Northwest – from Washington and Oregon specifically.

He didn't seem to care about disguising himself, boldly identifying himself as "Ted" to many women. His most often used 'bait and hook' ruse was to pretend to be injured. A broken arm, a cast, or crutches was how he gained women's sympathies. Pretending to have trouble managing with books or groceries, he would ask women for help with something in his car. Once there, the girls were pushed in, often knocked out, where they were trapped in his Volkswagen Beetle that had been modified to prevent escape.

In 1975, one woman, Carol DeRonch, escaped from his grasp, and he was later convicted of her kidnapping. Two years later, he escaped from prison, and was captured after 8 days. In December of 1977, he again escaped. On the night of January 14, 1978, he broke into the Chi Omega sorority house at Florida State University. Out of the four girls he attacked, two of them died.

On February 9, Bundy kidnapped and murdered Kimberly Leach, a 12-year-old girl from the area. He was pulled over by police, shortly after, and this finally ended his devastating killing career.

Law Enforcement believed Ted Bundy slaughtered upwards of 100 people.

Serial Killer John Wayne Gacy was a bi-sexual man who grew up in an abusive home. In his adult life, he raped and killed 33 young men and boys in Cook County, Illinois, burying them under the floorboards of his house. In public, he was a clown performer, and acted as a clown at children's parties. He was said to be a pillar in the community where he lived and was involved in a lot of social activities. While showing himself as that person to the general public, the truth was Gacy was baiting his murder victims with promises of construction work. Once in his home, he would drug them or ply them with alcohol. He would tie them up with a rope, torture and murder them.

In 1968, Gacy was convicted of sexually assaulting two teenage boys and sentenced to 10 years in prison. He was released on parole during the summer of 1970, and was arrested again in 1971 after another boy accused Gacy of sexual assault. The boy didn't show up for trial, so charges were dropped. By 1975, two more young men accused Gacy of rape. And he was questioned by police about the disappearance of others.

Robert Piest was 15 years old when he went missing in December of 1978. His mother reported that her son was last seen going to meet Gacy about a job. On December 21, police searched Gacy's house in Norwood Park Township, Illinois, and uncovered evidence of numerous heinous acts, including murder. It was noted that Gacy committed his first known killing in 1972, when he took the life of Timothy McCoy.

Serial Killer Dennis Rader, aka BTK (bind-torture-kill), was active in Wichita, Kansas from 1974 to 1991. He killed 10 people during his rampage. He was an impatient killer, and often taunted authorities with letters and phone calls.

As a child, Rader hung small animals and tortured others. As an adult, he worked for a security company, giving him access to many peoples' homes. Rader took advantage of this opportunity. His first known murder was on January 15, 1974, when he slaughtered four members of a family in their Wichita home...Joseph and Julie Otero and two of their children, Josephine and Joseph Jr. He strangled them all to death, and took a watch and a radio as souvenirs. It was reported he left semen at the scene, however, this was before DNA was used to solve crimes. Rader admitted he received sexual pleasure from both the killing and from the souvenirs afterward.

On the 30th anniversary, of the Otero murders, in 2004, BTK's ego got the best of him and he decided to seek attention from media and law enforcement. Rader sent local media outlets and authorities several letters along with items related to his crimes, including pictures, a word puzzle, and an outline for what he hoped would be his story - the "BTK Story." He also left packages with clues, including a computer disk that ultimately led authorities to Rader.

BTK was arrested in February 2005. The state of Kansas charged him with 10 counts of first-degree murder. His neighbors and the rest of the community were stunned by the news, unable to believe that the man they knew all this time was in fact the serial killer that preyed on the area for so long.

Serial Killer Edmund Kemper, known as "The Co-ed Killer," brutally murdered his grandparents when he was only 15, just to "see what it would feel like." He was diagnosed as a paranoid schizophrenic by mental health doctors, and remanded to the Atascadero State Hospital. In only five years, he was released as being rehabilitated. He was 20 years old.

Between May 1972 and April 1973, Kemper embarked on a murderous rampage that began with two college students and ended with the murders of his mother and her best friend.

Kemper started Community College and began to pick up girls who were hitchhiking. At first, he took them to their destinations, but the urge to kill was too strong. He began to pick them up and drive them to a secluded area instead. He would kill them there, drive them back to his house, have sex with their dead bodies, and then dismember them. Kemper killed five college students, one high school student, his mother and her best friend. It is widely accepted fact Kemper killed all of the girls because of his hatred for his mother; corroborated by the unspeakable acts he did to his mother after her death. It appeared he killed her friend only because she was so close to the woman he hated more than anything in the world. After killing his mother's friend, he called the police and confessed.

Once his mother was gone, he no longer had a need to kill.

Many other less-known serial killers were active in America during this time and inflicting their own version of terror, including:

- *Richard Cottingham*, who used the streets of New York and New Jersey to stalk and kill during the 1970s. He was known as "The Torso Killer" because he would sometimes butcher the body of his victims, leaving only their torso

- *Lawrence Sigmund Bittaker and Roy Lewis Norris*, were known as "The Tool Box Killers." Over a five-month period, they kidnapped, raped, tortured, and murdered five teenage girls in Southern California

- *David Carpenter*, aka "The Trailside Killer," attacked and killed five women on San Francisco area hiking trails between 1979 and 1981

- *Richard Chase* killed six people in the span of a month in Sacramento, California. He was nicknamed "The Vampire of Sacramento" after drinking his victims' blood and eating their remains

- *Dean Corll,* along with teenaged accomplices, *David Owen Brooks* and *Elmer Wayne Henley Jr* killed at least 28 boys in a series of killings spanning from 1970 to 1973 in Houston, Texas

- *Robert Christian Hansen* abducted, raped, and murdered at least 17 women in Alaska between 1971 and 1983. He hunted them down in the woods, after taking them there. He stalked them, sometimes with his airplane, and either shot them or stabbed them. He is thought to have killed up to 30 women

The reason for this widespread presence of serial killers during this time period is unknown, but there are dozens of theories. Forensics was nowhere near as advanced as it is today, and this encouraged those who had the desire, to go ahead and kill. The fear of being caught didn't exist like it does today. The media of that time, in many cases, became part of the story. Many serial killers taunted them with letters, phone calls, and photos. Crime is a social anomaly that reflects the time and place. And during that time, America had a cultural approval of hitch hiking, a vast road system that covered broad open spaces, and a more liberal perspective towards violence and sex.

Investigative reporter, Diane Dimond, reported on the establishment of the Behavioral Sciences Unit of the FBI:

"The FBI allowed a visionary special agent named Howard Teten to establish what would ultimately become the Behavioral Sciences Unit. Teten devised a groundbreaking analytical approach, now known as psychological criminal profiling, to try to identify unknown killers."

Teten's agents dedicated themselves to studying high-volume kill areas around the country and meticulously linked similarities between the cases. They analyzed the lifestyle, physical attributes, and location of victims. They looked at the methods the killers used to commit their murders, and exactly how they left their victims. Patterns emerged. There was a swath of the country where pretty brunette co-eds were repeatedly reported missing. Some hospitals experienced an extraordinary number of unexplained deaths. Bodies were found with similar and unique wound patterns. Victims had been left in similar provocative positions. All similarities were put together like pieces of a big ugly puzzle. Agents began to know the 'how' and 'where' of multiple murders, but not the 'who'.

Although the exact date is unknown, this is around the time the FBI began to use the term "serial killer" as opposed to the less precise "murder without motive" designation they used before that.

My research also led to a startling revelation – 1974 was the year in which several of America's most notorious and prolific serial killers began their reigns of bloody terror.

Ted Bundy committed his first murder in January 1974.

Dennis Rader first murdered in January 1974.

John Wayne Gacy killed the second of his 34 victims in January 1974.

Coral Eugene Watts murdered the first of an estimated 90 victims in 1974.

Paul John Knowles went on a killing spree, murdering 18 people in 1974.

Coincidence? Or, what was it about 1974?

Also, in 1974, the FBI first became aware of the murderous maniac, Zodiac, active in San Francisco. Someone else was systematically picking up military men who were home on leave in Southern California, dumping their dismembered bodies along major highways.

Retired FBI special agent Jim Clemente worked in the FBI's Behavioral Analysis Unit (the modern-day name of Agent Teten's original BSU) for his entire 22-year career at the Bureau. He said, *"At the time the BAU had no idea how devastating a year 1974 would turn out to be. Some of the most brilliant and prolific serial killers would launch their destructive careers at that time. But it would be decades before they were all brought to justice."*

As FBI agents were building their multiple puzzles, the elusive Bundy would murder upwards of 36 people over the next four years. Dennis Rader killed until 1991. Gacy wouldn't be caught until late 1978. Watts continued his bloody spree for more than eight years. Thankfully, Knowles was on a rapid path of destruction and his career in murder ended after five months when a police officer shot and killed him.

Sure, there were news reports about some of these murders and missing people left behind in the frenzy of serial killing. But in 1974, the nation's attention was scattered. The Vietnam War was still ongoing, there was a frantic worldwide nuclear arms race underway, the Watergate Scandal was toppling the administration of President Richard Nixon, and the daughter of multi-millionaire Randolph Hearst was kidnapped. Because of all this, most Americans didn't notice that the nation's homicide rate was soaring.

But the FBI knew. They knew the murderous score and worried about creating public panic. So, they kept the information quiet. The lesson learned from this look back at history is that since that peak of serial killing madness in the 1970s and 1980s (603 serial killers identified during that time), the numbers have decreased every single decade since. In the 1990s, there were 498 known serial killers. In 2000, there were 371, and in 2010, there were 117. It's a testament to the perseverance of the FBI and to all law enforcement that studied and implemented Special Agent Teten's revolutionary criminal profiling protocol.

Chapter 2: Rodney Alcala

Hiding in the shadows of depravity, probably the most cunning and terrifying of all serial killers was Rodney James Alcala. He flew 'under the radar' and was able to travel easily from east to west coast of the United States during his murderous career. But what made him so frightening was the fact that he was smart. Really smart. He was said to have a genius IQ. And not only was he handsome, it was said he was hypnotic to women. He didn't have to search for victims. Women actually came to him. With his charm and good looks, he was able to hide like a snake in the grass and strike with the precision of a cobra. And because of his charm and good looks, he was able to easily set a trap for young, beautiful girls and women. He dressed and groomed himself like someone important, and women flocked to him.

Rodney Alcala fancied himself a photographer, and he used his photography skills to the fullest. He was able to lure his victims into secluded locations and vulnerable situations with the promise of their being 'discovered.' After all, this was the dream of many young women in the seventies.

Rodney James Alcala was born on August 23, 1943, in San Antonio, Texas, and given the name Rodrigo Jacques Alcala-Buquor. His Mexican parents were Raoul Alcala-Buquor and Anna Maria Gutierrez. He had an older brother, Raoul, and older sister Marie Therese. He also had a younger sister, Marie Christine, born when he was almost four years old. When Alcala was 11 or 12 years old, his father left the family, and his mother moved the children to Los Angeles.

Alcala graduated from public high school, Montebello High, in 1960. On June 19, 1961, he entered a program in North Carolina to become a paratrooper. He enlisted in the U.S Army where he served as a clerk for four years. In 1963, when he was 20 years old, he showed up at his mother's door unexpectedly. He hitchhiked from Fort Bragg, travelling about three thousand miles to go AWOL.

In early 1964, he was medically discharged from the U.S. Army after having a reported nervous breakdown. He was diagnosed with an antisocial personality disorder, chronic, and severe. When he was released from the hospital, he returned to his mother's Los Angeles home. Interestingly, his military record has been wiped clean and no information was available.

From 1964 to 1968, Alcala lived in California and attended UCLA. He graduated with a Bachelor of Arts degree in 1968. Not much else is known about what he did during these years. His first known attack occurred on September 25, 1968, and his attacks progressed in frequency, and in severity, until he killed his last victim in 1979.

* Author's Note: Law enforcement believes Alcala's attack in 1968 was his first crime. I, however, doubt that it was. Law enforcement has also expressed the belief that Alcala killed upwards of 100 people while he was active. I believe this to be a minimum.

Chapter 3: Tali Shapiro

"She did not know that the wolf was a wicked sort of animal.

And she was not afraid of him."

- Little Red Riding Hood

Tali Shapiro hurried as she walked along Sunset Boulevard in Hollywood, California. It was September 25, 1968. She was only 8 years old, but she was old enough to know she was going to be late for school. She alternated between walking and running as she made her way to her destination as quickly as she could. She attended Gardner Street Elementary and liked school. Her favorite was playing dodgeball, and she was probably thinking of that, and not contemplating her surroundings all that much. She hadn't noticed the beige-colored car that had passed her twice already, slowing down next to her, and pulling over. A man's voice, sounding almost like her dad, called out to her to get in and he would give her a ride to school. She turned to look at him and saw that his windows were down. He was smiling at her. She wondered, briefly, if she might know him. But then she realized that although he looked familiar to her, she didn't recognize him. Her parents told her never talk to strangers. This bright child told the man that she was not supposed to talk to strangers.

Tali felt a rush of relief as he told her that he wasn't a stranger because her parents were friends of his. As he drove slowly along next to her, the friendly man began asking her questions. He asked her if she liked art class in school. When she said that she did, he told her that he had a beautiful picture to show her.

She was relieved that not only did this smiling man know her parents but also that he was going to show her a beautiful picture. And he was going to give her a ride to school. They drove for a while and she felt a slight pang of anxiety that maybe she should not have gotten into the car. Because she was a sweet and trusting little girl, the feeling quickly passed with thoughts of seeing beautiful fields with bouncy animals in the picture he talked about. She could never imagine that an adult would hurt her. She trusted adults! No adult had ever hurt her. He also reminded her that because he was going to drive her to school, she wouldn't be late if they just stopped quickly at his apartment.

Donald Haines, an alert man traveling the same route that morning, noticed a man in a beige car that seemed to be stalking the child. He immediately knew that something was wrong. He witnessed the brief encounter between the man in the vehicle and the little girl. He couldn't believe the child had climbed into the car. Something made him follow them to their destination on De Longpre Avenue in Hollywood. Haines watched as they exited the car, noticing the little girl seemed to be reluctant as the man hurried her up the stairs into his apartment. Haines felt uneasy as he looked for a pay phone to alert the police.

When Officer Chris Camacho arrived at the dispatched address, no one answered the door the first time he knocked. He knocked a second time and announced, "LA Police. Open the door. I want to talk to you."

A man appeared from behind the blinds, saying he had just taken a shower and would be right out. The officer noticed the man seemed very nervous and wasn't wet from a shower.

Camacho waited briefly, but when he heard a sound coming from the other side of the door that sounded like moaning, the hair on the back of his neck stood up. He shouted, "Open the door now, or I'm kicking it in."

Other officers arrived, and by the time they kicked the door in, the man that Camacho seen had escaped through another door and was gone. Officers looked through the house, finding a lot of photographic equipment, and piles of photographs of young girls. Camacho entered the kitchen and found the little girl, nude and lying in a pool of blood. She was on her back, unconscious, with her legs spread apart. Her head was smashed open and a large, steel bar was across her neck. The beautiful child was battered, bleeding, but amazingly, still alive. It was agonizing to see the little dress, socks, and shoes thrown around her tiny body. Camacho's training quickly told him to remove the bar away from the child's neck, and check for a pulse. Although she looked dead, he was able to feel a slight pulse. Urgently, he called for an ambulance. Tali was rushed to the hospital in a critical state.

Fortunately, Tali didn't remember much past going into the apartment and looking at a picture. Alcala hit her over the head as soon as they got inside and split her head open. She was mercifully unconscious to his ruthless attack.

Tali Shapiro survived the attack with 27 stitches in the back of her head and a month-long hospital stay. However, she suffered a lifetime of recovery from going through an experience that no one should ever have to go through, much less an innocent, 8-year-old child. The brutalization of Tali Shapiro became the first known crime of Rodney Alcala.

Chapter 4: FBI Warrant

"And I thought, 'One for the good guys.' She's gonna make it."
— Officer Chris Camacho

Forty-two years later, the television show "48 Hours Mystery," brought the story of Rodney Alcala and his attack on Tali Shapiro to television. This is the actual report from the first officer, Chris Camacho, on scene that day:

"I was out doing my patrols. We just started our shift that day. I was driving down Sunset Boulevard, and I had received a call, "Los Angeles Police Officer, Chris Camacho recalled of that September morning in 1968. "A beige colored car with no license plates was following this little girl."

"I went to that location," Camacho recalls. "And I started knocking. I said, "Police officer. Open the door. I need to talk to you."

This male appeared at the door. "I will always remember that face at the door" —very evil face.

"And he says, 'I'm in the shower. I gotta get dressed.' I told him 'OK. You got 10 seconds. Open this door I want to talk to you.' Finally, I kicked the door in.

"The image will be with me forever. We could see in the kitchen there was a body on the floor, a lot of blood."

"They say a picture says a thousand words, and that image of those little white Mary Janes on that floor with that metal bar that he used to strangle her with and that puddle of blood, it just looks like too much blood to come out of a tiny little 8-year-old like that."

"She had been raped. There was no breathing. I thought she was dead. We all thought she was dead," Camacho recalls. "So I grabbed a towel, and I picked up the edge of the bar and I - I laid it off to the side."

"We started searching the residence… there was a lot of photograph equipment," Camacho continues.

"All of us were amazed at the amount of photographs he had there of young girls, very young girls."

"We found – a lot of ID, picture ID of a Rodney Alcala. He was a student at UCLA – an undergrad student."

"Unfortunately," Camacho explains, *"the other officers – when I kicked the front door – came running around to assist me and – the suspect went out the back door."*

But moments later, when Camacho walked back into the kitchen where Tali was, he witnessed a miracle.

"She was gagging and trying to breathe. And I thought, 'One for the good guys.' She's gonna make it."

Tali was immediately rushed to the hospital.

"When I was in Vietnam, and we were in combat I was trying to save this guy and didn't do it. He died. So with Tali, it was kind of like God gave me a second chance to save someone."

Soon after Tali healed, her parents moved her out of the country.

"I found out that they had moved to Mexico, that they did not wanna raise their daughter in this society any longer. And that was the last I heard of them," says Camacho.

Alcala had escaped and it was now up to the investigators in Los Angeles to find him. There were stories about him living in Mexico, Canada, and even Europe. But none of their leads panned out. Forensic science was not the crime-solving weapon it is today. Also, there was resistance with those who knew him. A lot of people were unwilling to believe Alcala, who was praised as a gifted student, could have committed this heinous act on a child. One of Alcala's professors stated that he "wouldn't harm a fly."

Unable to find him, the FBI put Alcala on their Most Wanted List in 1969.

Chapter 5: Cornelia Crilley

"I crossed the street to her house and she opened the door.

She stood there laughing
I felt the knife in my hand and she laughed no more"

– "Delilah" by Tom Jones

Alcala's first known murder occurred on June 12, 1971. He brutally raped Cornelia Crilley, strangling her with her nylon stockings and leaving her dead in her apartment in New York City. The 23-year-old was a Trans World Airlines flight attendant and had just moved into a new apartment. The two might have met when Alcala saw Crilley moving furniture into her new apartment. Perhaps he offered to help. We will never know.

Cornelia was found behind the locked doors of her apartment, leaning up against an overturned bed. There was a rope around her neck and her bra had been pulled up. There were bite marks on her left breast. Authorities worked her case relentlessly, but were not able to come up with any suspects. In time, the case went cold.

News article from "The Bridgeport Post" on June 26, 1971:

"Police conducted an intensive manhunt today in the Yorkville section of Manhattan, seeking the killer of an airline stewardess found strangled in her apartment Thursday night.

A team of 25 detectives was scouring the neighborhood for clues concerning the murder of Cornelia Michelle Crilley, 23, a stewardess for Trans World Airlines.

Miss Crilley's partially clad body was found in an apartment on East 83rd Street that she recently had rented to share with two other young women.

Police said Miss Crilley had been sexually molested and then strangled.

The search for the killer took policeman to neighbors and to the "singles bars" that accommodate the many young single people who live in the East Side community.

TWA offered a $5,000 reward for information leading to capture of the killer.

Police discounted robbery a motive for the attack. The door to the apartment was locked, leading police to theorize that the killer locked it with Miss Crilley's key upon leaving.

Miss Crilley's two roommates were away, and she was known to be moving furniture into the apartment. No screams or other untoward sounds were heard by neighbors," police said.

"The possibility that a man hired by the stewardess to help with the furniture killed her is being considered by the police.

Miss Crilley has been with the airline since graduating from airline stewardess school about 18 months ago."

It wasn't until years later, in 2011, when DNA found at the crime scene would conclusively prove that Rodney Alcala murdered Cornelia Crilley. And in January 2013, Alcala was extradited to New York to face the charges.

Chapter 6: Girl Camp

"Oh yes I'm the great pretender
Adrift in a world of my own
I play the game but to my real shame
You've left me to dream all alone

Too real is this feeling of make believe
Too real when I feel what my heart can't conceal"

– "The Great Pretender" by The Platters

when he escaped the scene of his savage attempted murder of 8-year-old Tali Shapiro, he fled east to New York. He used the name John Berger to enroll in NYU film school. It appears from 1968 to 1971, he was able to move freely about the country, unrecognized, even though he was on the FBI's Most Wanted List. During this time, Alcala frequented New York's clubs, meeting young women, and playing the role of the photographer. He took hundreds of photos of young women, outside on the street, inside clubs, and in his apartment.

On August 12, 1971, Alcala was arrested in New Hampshire. He was working as a counselor at "New Beginnings," an all-girls summer camp near Lake Sunapee for the last three summers under a slightly different alias, "John Burger." One day, two girls from the camp were in the Post Office in the little town of Georges Mills. They had stepped inside to get out of a sudden summer downpour.

They eyed the FBI posters of Most Wanted people and were shocked to see that a photo of a man named "Rodney Alcala" looked very much like their camp counselor, John Burger. This man, Alcala, had hurt a little girl in California.

The girls notified the director of the camp and he went down to check up on the poster. When he realized the man in the photo was indeed the same man working at the camp, he called the FBI. Alcala was arrested and extradited to California to face charges for what he had done.

* Author's Note: Alcala was known to be in the New York/New Hampshire area from September 1968 to August 1971. Knowing what I know about Alcala, I strongly believe he was carrying on his murderous deeds during this time, in either New Hampshire, or nearby states. Any missing women during this time would be a possibility of having been a victim of Alcala.

After extradition, when questioned by an investigator about Tali Shapiro, he simply responded, "I want to forget all about that. I don't wanna talk about the things that Rod Alcala did."

Alcala was convicted in March 1972 for the brutal attack on Tali Shapiro. The Shapiro family had relocated to Mexico for the comfort and safety of their little girl. They refused to allow her to testify at Alcala's trial. Without her testimony, the prosecutors were unable to convict him of rape and attempted murder. They were forced to let Alcala plead guilty of the lesser charge of assault. Less than three years into his sentence, he was able to charm the psychiatric staff into saying he was "greatly improved," with their recommendation he be released. In 1974, he was set free.

Alcala went home to live with his mother in southern California. There, he had access to a vehicle, and his own room with a private entrance. This cunning monster had it made once again. His mother didn't question anything he did, and his family seemed to protect him from any legal ramifications.

* Author's Note: No record is available of his activities between August 3, 1974 and October 16, 1974. This is another probable period of time where he could have attacked and/or killed women. Any women or children, who went missing during this period of time, could possibly be his victims. He was staying on the west coast; however, short travels to the surrounding states would be possible for him.

Chapter 7: Julie Johnson

On October 16, 1974, thirteen-year-old Julie Johnson, waited for a bus to take her to school in Huntington Beach. A man approached her and introduced himself as "John Ronald." They spoke briefly but it was long enough for him to convince her to accept a ride to school.

Once in the car, he asked how old she was. She told him she was thirteen but people usually thought she was younger. He told her that she would like that when she was older. When he passed her school, she pointed it out. But he didn't stop. He continued down towards Pacific Coast Highway, ignoring Julie's requests to go to her school.

Julie began to scream but he yelled at her to shut up. She tried to get out of the car several times while they were moving but he grabbed her arm. Once they stopped, she tried again to escape him. He dragged her from the car to a spot along the bluffs overlooking the ocean at Huntington Beach. He offered her marijuana. Julie had never smoked before, but because she was afraid, she agreed.

When she passed it back to him, she dropped it. As he reached for it, she made another attempt to run. He grabbed her leg and pulled her close to him. He gave her a deep French kiss and asked her, "Are you passionate when you are loaded?"

Fortunately for Julie, a park ranger walking the trail below noticed them. The ranger thought they were probably up to no good, so he walked up to them. When asked what they were doing, Alcala said they were hiking and were just taking a break. Julie blurted out that she had been taken there against her will, and she wanted to go home. Alcala was immediately put into handcuffs. Both were put into the car, each telling the ranger different stories. A background check revealed Alcala's past criminal history. He was booked on several counts, including violating parole, possession of marijuana, and kidnapping. He was convicted and sentenced to two and a half years on December 26, 1975.

A mere year and half later in June 1977, Alcala came up for parole, and once again was declared 'reformed.' All he had to do was report to a parole officer once a week and he was on his way.

True to his nature, Alcala manipulated his parole officer into allowing him to visit relatives across the country in New York City.

Chapter 8: Ellen Hover

Alcala wasn't even in New York a week when he murdered Ellen Hover. Hover was a Manhattan socialite and piano prodigy. Her father was Herman Hover, a well-known businessman. Relatives later said that she was a sweet and naive young woman.

She would have found it exciting that a 'real' photographer wanted to take photos of her.

A friend reported that on July 13, 1977 she saw Ellen talking to a tall man with a ponytail outside her apartment building. Ellen told the friend that he was a photographer and wanted to take photos of her. They had set up a lunch date for July 15. When she didn't return home that day, her parents called the police. Police found nothing suspicious when they went into her apartment and everything seemed to be in order. The name "John Berger" was discovered, written in her calendar on the day she went missing.

The NYPD continued to look for "John Berger," but Alcala was already on his way back to Los Angeles.

The skeletal remains of 23-year-old Ellen Hover were found 11 months later at the Rockefeller estate in suburban Westchester County. They were found spread all over the brush on the acreage.

It would be over three decades before law enforcement were able to piece together that Rodney Alcala and John Berger were one in the same.

In December of 1977, the FBI called the LAPD to discuss the disappearance of Ellen Hover. They were looking for John Berger. When they discovered John Berger was another alias for Rodney Alcala, they brought him in for questioning.

They asked him about Ellen Hover and were shocked when he admitted to knowing her. They were also shocked when he admitted he was with her on the day she went missing. He said they were friends and would often go out to take photos together. Alcala admitted they had done that on the day she went missing, but he insisted he had left her safely at her door, and didn't have a clue what happened to her. They asked him if he would take a polygraph, but he declined.

At this point in time, they didn't even have a body, so they had to release him. It would be years before DNA would conclusively prove he killed Ellen Hover. In January 2013, Alcala was extradited to New York, where he faced the murder charges of Cornelia Crilley (1971) and Ellen Hover (1977).

Chapter 9: Christine Thornton

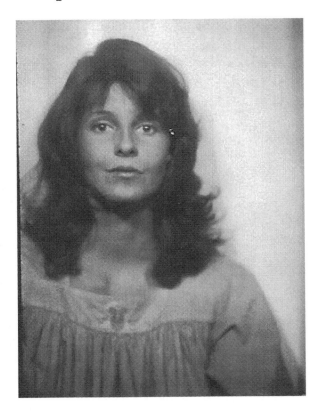

Also in the summer of 1977, Alcala murdered Christine Ruth Thornton and dumped her body in a remote area northeast of Granger, Wyoming. It is believed the two met somewhere in Wyoming, Thornton was 28 years old and six months pregnant at the time of her death.

On April 6, 1982, a rancher on remote, public land, northeast of Granger, Wyoming, in Sweetwater County, uncovered Christine's remains. Her DNA was taken and her remains were listed in "The Doe Network." (See Appendix B) Sadly, Christine remained a 'Jane Doe' until 2013, when a family member saw her photo among the unidentified photos released by Huntington Beach Police in 2010. The family member's DNA matched and Christine was officially identified in 2015.

Because the photographs were hidden from the public until 2010, family members were never able to view them. In 2013, Christine's sister, Kathy Thornton, recognized her sister in a photograph within the gallery. Christine was sitting on a Kawasaki 500 motorcycle, wearing a bright yellow shirt, smiling at the photographer. We now know the photographer was Rodney Alcala and he took her life shortly after. When authorities found Christine's remains, the yellow shirt was with her body.

Prosecutors in Rock Springs, Wyoming, made an announcement in September 2016, confirming Rodney Alcala had met Christine Ruth Thornton of San Antonio, TX, and he killed her on a road trip to Wyoming in 1977. They further stated they were charging him with her murder. Alcala admitted he had taken the photo of Christine, but said he didn't kill her.

Alcala would not stand trial for Thornton's murder. He was physically unable to travel, due to a medical condition. Apparently, he was unable to walk or leave the medical facility that housed him. Based on this information, Sweetwater County Attorney Daniel Erramouspe decided not to extradite him.

"The fact that this case will not be proven in court does nothing to dissuade me from knowing that Alcala murdered Ms. Thornton," Erramouspe said in a press release. *"The solving of this cold case, with the random facts, indicates solid investigation and integrity by the Sweetwater County Sheriff's Office, especially, Detective Jeff Sheaman, along with Sgt. Joe Tomich and Lt. John Grossnickle. It also shows the power of perseverance on behalf of Ms. Thornton's family, in never giving up the search for their sister."*

Chapter 10: Pamela Lambson

Few who are aware of the deviancy and patterns of Rodney Alcala believe that he didn't commit any attacks or murders between the Summer of 1977 (when he murdered Hover and Thornton) and November of 1977 (when he killed Jill Barcomb). Since he was in Wyoming in the summer, it is not only possible, but also very likely, there were other victims along the way.

From the murder of Ellen Hover in June 1977, to his last murder of Robin Samsoe in June of 1979, he was attacking and murdering women once a month. The only reprieve the public had from this monster was a couple of months here and there for drug arrests. Because of the timing and how she was murdered, authorities believe Alcala was responsible for the murder of 19-year-old Pamela Jean Lambson on October 8, 1977.

Pamela Lambson was eager to be famous and longed to be part of the entertainment industry. She had everything it took to become a success. She just needed that 'big break.' So when the charming freelance photographer, Rodney Alcala, asked her to take pictures for him, she was enthusiastic and had no second thoughts about it.

Looking quite professional, Alcala wore his long hair pulled back in a ponytail that day. Pamela didn't suspect anything other than to perhaps be discovered. She wore a new dress and peacock feather earrings. "This may be my big chance," she told a friend, according to published accounts.

Her nude and beaten body was found on a trail on Mount Tamalpais the next day. She had been tortured and strangled.

The Lambson homicide has been a cold case for 30 years, but the Marin Sheriff's Department believe that Rodney Alcala was the freelance photographer who met with Lambson that day. The case is currently listed as "inactive with a known suspect."

Chapter 11: Jill Barcomb

Early in the morning of November 10, 1977, West Los Angeles police were called to a scene in a rugged and remote area off Franklin Canyon Drive.

They received a call for an ambulance and were notified that a dead body might be in the area. As the officers took in the abhorrent setting, they saw a young woman on the ground. She was on all fours with her knees bent. Her inner thighs and knees pointed outward; she was not wearing any panties. Her buttocks were spread wide, and her anus was lacerated. Her head was on the ground, tucked tightly against her breasts. The top of her head was forced between her knees, touching the ground. Blood pooled in the dirt below as it had poured from her vagina and anus. Her clothing, a green and orange sweater and pants, were nearby. Blood soaked her clothes, and one pant leg was tied around her neck. A pool of blood encircled her head, and a 7" x 5" x 3" blood-soaked rock with a sharp point was in the middle of it. There were footprints facing toward the body.

The Jane Doe #95 autopsy report stated the devastation that was done to the young woman:

"Massive face, head, and neck trauma, including deep cuts embedded with broken bone fragments into her skull.

Blood seepage all around her brain.

Small blood vessels in her eye and all around her heart ruptured from pressure and the deprivation of oxygen.

Three ligatures around her neck: a top ligature of her blood-soaked left pant leg tied into a granny knot up under her left ear; a middle ligature of two knee high nylons, knotted together, and tied around her neck; a bottom ligature of a woman's belt cranked tight around her neck.

A deep bite mark surrounding the nearly severed nipple of her right breast.

Four blood smears, like four fingers, "where the offender was holding the breast while he was biting the nipple."

Blood smears all over the body where the assailant was "manhandling and twisting and pulling and doing whatever."

Deep scratch marks, indicating defensive injuries, on her arms, shoulders, pelvic area and abdomen.

Multiple bleeding lacerations and cuts penetrating her anus.

Singed pubic hair."

In the autopsy report, it stated:

"The body was that of a female, four feet eleven inches tall, weighing around ninety-five pounds.

Almost all of her injuries were inflicted while she was still alive and blood was pumping through her body. She was strangled with hands, then with ligatures, then bashed on the head. The beatings to her head were antemortem (before death): She was definitely alive.

The impact of the blows to the head were consistent with that from a rock.

There were multiple causes of death: blunt force trauma to the head and to the neck, either of which could have killed her; with strangulation being a contributing cause."

The young woman was 18-year-old Jill Barcomb. She had only recently moved to Los Angeles from Oneida, New York.

At first, law enforcement believed that Jill might have been a victim of The Hillside Strangler – an alias for the killing cousin duo, Kenneth Bianchi and Angelo Buono. They were also active at the time, kidnapping, raping, torturing, and killing women during a four-month period in 1977 and 1978. Their crimes took place in the "Hills" above Los Angeles.

To discover that this was not a crime committed by the Hillside Strangler must have been a shock for law enforcement. How could it be possible that there was more than one man who was savagely attacking women in the Los Angeles area?

Similar to the other murders, it wasn't until years later, in 2011, when DNA found at the crime scene would conclusively prove that Rodney Alcala murdered Jill Barcomb.

Chapter 12: Georgia Wixted

On the morning of December 16, 1977, Los Angeles County Sheriff's Department received a request to check on the welfare of Georgia Wixted, a 27-year-old nurse. A co-worker had called to report that Georgia had not showed up that morning to give her a ride to work. In fact, Georgia had not called in sick or turned up for work at all that day.

Deputies went to the address on Pacific Coast Highway and found her ground level apartment. They immediately noticed there was a screen missing from one of the windows of her apartment. Under the window with the missing screen, was a box one might step up on to get inside. The officers knocked on the door, but no one answered. Trying the front door, they found it was open. They entered the apartment and immediately saw Wixted on the floor. Once other officers arrived, they took in details of the horrible scene: Georgia Wixted was naked, lying on her back, lacerations covered her body, blood and dark bruising were showing everywhere on her skin. Her knees were posed, pointed outward, and there was blood between her legs. Her neck was wrapped tightly with a pair of pantyhose. They saw a large, dark blood stain in the middle of her mattress. Her bedding and nightshirt was strewn around the room, and covered in blood. All four walls of the bedroom had blood spatter, as well as substantial amounts in the bathroom. Blood was found on the toilet seat, on a bar of soap, a towel rack, and the walls. A claw hammer, coated with blood, was found next to the victim's head.

The coroner performed an autopsy on December 18, 1977. He recorded her substantial injuries:

"Massive face and head trauma; including circular bruises, skull fractures, and claw-like lacerations into her skull.

Tears inside the front part of her mouth and lower lip from blunt-force impact.

Cut marks on her neck from ligatures and broken bones inside her neck and under her jaw, which had pierced through to the back of her throat from the force applied to tightening the ligatures.

Ruptured blood vessels in her eyes from the pressure to her neck.

A fractured and dislocated arm.

Lacerations of the lips of the vagina and labia."

The coroner concluded that:

"Almost every injury was inflicted while she was alive and blood was still pumping through the body.

Ligature marks to the neck were consistent with strangulation, and a tear to the vaginal wall was consistent with forced penetration by an object.

The fracture to the left skull was consistent with being struck by a hammer.

A palm print from the brass railing of the bed was recovered, as was the sperm from inside her vaginal, anal, and oral cavities."

Alcala was not linked to Wixted's murder until many years later because DNA technology was not available in 1977. But in 2011, DNA conclusively proved that Alcala was the one who committed the murder.

On March 22, 1978, Alcala was questioned at his mother's home in Monterey Park, California, as part of the Hillside Strangler investigation. Even before Alcala was positively identified as a serial killer, he was at least on law enforcement's radar. But the dots weren't connected yet.

During the interview, he was discovered to be in possession of marijuana and sent back to jail for a short period. The dates were not noted, but in May or June of 1978, Alcala was once again out on the streets of Los Angeles stalking new victims.

Chapter 13: Charlotte Lamb

In the early morning hours of June 24, 1978, a resident of an apartment complex in El Segundo, decided to get up early to do his laundry. When he arrived at the laundry room, he saw something he could barely believe he was seeing – a nude female, lying face up on the concrete, with blood all around her. She had been posed to appear in a bizarre and frightening position.

The apartment manager made a call to Los Angeles County Sheriff's Department about the body discovered in the laundry room. The deputies arrived around 11:15 a.m. Along with everything else that had been reported, the deputies noticed a long shoelace wrapped tightly around her neck, still attached to a sandal. The sandal hung next to her head.

Her arms were pulled awkwardly behind her back, propping up her breasts. Her legs were spread wide and faced the doorway of the laundry room, so she would be seen immediately by anyone entering the room. The murderer staged her for the ultimate shock and awe. There was extensive trauma to her head and face, and a bloody piece of wood was near her body.

The shoelace ligature was wrapped so tightly around her neck that her voice box and thyroid was crushed. Her neck, breasts, and shoulders had bite marks. There were injuries around the genital area, and hemorrhaging around the rim of her anus from either a penis or foreign object.

The apartment manager, who arrived at the scene after being notified by the resident, advised the police that the woman did not live in the complex. She had been brought there and murdered.

Charlotte Lamb had not been seen or heard from in several days. On her thirty-second birthday, her family reported her missing after they were unable to contact her. Police were able to match her with the body found in the laundry room of nearby apartments. It was speculated that either she was forced, or went willingly, into Alcala's vehicle, taken to the laundry room, and murdered.

Alcala was not linked to Charlotte Lamb's murder until many years later. In 2011, DNA conclusively proved that Alcala was the one who committed the murder.

By now, Alcala was in full swing of his murderous frenzy, and his desire to kill was out of control.

Chapter 14: The Dating Game

In September of 1978, the television show, "The Dating Game," was one of the most popular on TV. Despite the fact that Alcala was a registered sex offender and convicted rapist, he was selected as a contestant for the show. He was introduced as Bachelor Number One – a successful photographer, and the audience cheered for him.

He appeared relaxed, with a beaming smile. His hair was dark and fell in curls to his shoulders. He wore a dark leisure suit and a crisp white shirt. He owned the stage and easily won the date. The Bachelorette, Cheryl Bradshaw, was excited to meet him. Fortunately for Bradshaw, they never went on that date.

While watching the video of the program, it was easy to see how frightening a man Alcala was with his cheesy answers to the Bachelorette, Cheryl Bradshaw. (*__Watch the video here https://rjpp.ca/RODNEY-ALCALA__*)

Some people said that Alcala went on his killing spree because he was turned down by Bradshaw. But in a letter written to a fan years later (see below), it didn't seem as if it mattered all that much to him. It appeared he and Bradshaw both had significant others in their lives.

... -- --- .auie magazines, so I can't
pick one that I'd like to have.
As for studying under Roman Polanski, he did have
a class at UCLA which I took in the 1960's; although
I don't have any particular memory of him or
his class. My favorite 35mm camera now would
probably be a Nikon. Right now, it's been so long
since I had a camera, that I can't recall what 35mm
camera I had; and that was my favorite camera.
then. That's nice, to have your girlfriend Debbie
in your Band; and that you've played all over the
world. The only parts of the world I've been are
Mexico, and western Europe. The only hobbies I have
now are going to the yard every day, and jogging;
doing 1,000 miles each year; and creating picture
magazines from pictures in the magazines I receive.
My day: 1. Doing one hour of my favorite exercises
starting around midnight; going to the yard, which is
available for 2-3 hours daily -- I jog, do pullups,
play Scrabble, and talk with the inmates in my yard.
I didn't actually get a date with the girl from the
"Dating Game." We both decided that we'd go our
way; her with her boyfriend, and me with my
girlfriend. No, you're not asking too many questions.
My favorite musics are rock and Mexican. And I only
follow politics that affect my encarceration. Well,
that's about it for now.

Sincerely,
Rodney

Rodney

"As for studying under Roman Polanski, he did have a class at UCLA which I took in the 1960's; although I don't have any particular memory of him or his class. My favorite 35mm camera now would probably be a Nikon. Right now,

it's been so long since I had a camera, that I can't recall what 35mm camera I had; and that was my favorite camera then. That's nice, to have your girlfriend Debbie in your Band; and that you've played all over the world. The only parts of the world I've been are Mexico, and western Europe. The only hobbies I have now are going to the yard every day, and jogging; doing 1,000 miles each year; and creating picture magazines from pictures in the magazines I receive. My day: 1. Doing one hour of my favorite exercises starting around midnight; going to the yard, which is available for 2-3 hours daily – I jog, do pullups, play Scrabble, and talk with the inmates in my yard. I didn't actually get a date with the girl from "The Dating Game." We both decided that we'd go our way: her with her boyfriend, and me with my girlfriend. No, you aren't asking too many questions. My favorite musics are rock and Mexican. And I only follow politics that affect my incarceration. Well, that's about it for now.

Sincerely,

Rodney"

* Author's Note: There is another five months gap, from September 1978 until February 1979, where Alcala's whereabouts are unaccounted for. Again, it is very doubtful that he stopped killing at the height of his rampage. Most likely, he was traveling to other areas to

search for his prey, Given his track record, it is inconceivable that these months were not prime killing months. He was known to travel all over the United States. All women missing during these months need to be considered as his potential victims.

Chapter 15: Monique Hoyt

Pasadena, a suburb of Los Angeles, is where fifteen-year-old Monique Hoyt met Rodney Alcala hitchhiking on February 13, 1979. Alcala pulled up next to her, with his broad, bright smile, and asked if she wanted to pose for some photos. He said there was a contest he wanted to enter, and was sure they would win. Besides the fact she needed a ride, she couldn't help but be flattered he thought she was attractive enough to win a contest. She jumped in the car, looking around to see a lot of photography equipment. She was very at ease to be there.

Alcala told her he needed to go to his mother's house to get some more equipment. It was late by the time they got there, so too dark to take outside photos. She decided to spend the night there with him.

In the morning, they drove to a deserted spot, about 80 miles away from downtown Los Angeles. Hoyt believed he must have known a good place to take photos, and didn't worry about the distance.

They walked for about 15 minutes, deep into the woods. He continued to chat with her, and there were no red flags as far as she was concerned. Hoyt didn't have a problem with posing naked, and he took many nude shots of her the evening before. All of a sudden, Alcala hit her over the head with a large tree branch. She blacked out. When she eventually came to, she stayed very still, pretending to be still out cold.

He began to bite her genital area and her breasts. Somehow, she was able to remain still while this was all going on. He penetrated her and sodomized her. She was only fifteen, and had not experienced this kind of pain and terror before. She stayed as still as she could, for as long as she could, but finally, the agony was too much, and she began screaming. This infuriated him, so he stuffed her T-shirt into her mouth as he screamed at her to shut up.

Alcala choked her with his hands until she was unconscious again. She awakened a short time later. Her wrists and ankles were now tied with rope, and she was unable to move. She was able to peek through one eye and see he was lying on the ground next to her. He was sobbing.

This brave girl made a decision right then that saved her life. She rolled toward him, and pretended to be worried about him. She asked him if he was okay, speaking softly and kindly. She knew her only hope of getting out alive was making him believe she liked him and considered him a friend.

In 1979, the term 'reverse psychology' was not as popular a term as it is today. But, for whatever reason, that is what saved Monique Hoyt's life. She asked him never to tell anyone about what happened between them. After a few minutes, he untied her. He allowed her to dress and they walked back to the car.

On their way back, Alcala stopped to buy a soda and to use the restroom. She promised to wait for him, but as soon as he closed the door on the bathroom, she bolted from the car. She ran towards a motel next to the gas station, screaming she had been raped. She begged for someone to call the police. One of the guests at the hotel called the police and another took her into their room for safety. By the time the police arrived, he escaped. Hoyt was terribly beaten, raped, and sodomized, and understandably, hysterical. But she was still able to give authorities a description of her attacker. She was taken to the hospital, where they treated her injuries. From a photo line-up, she was able to identify Rodney Alcala as her attacker.

Alcala was arrested at his mother's house later that day and taken to the station. He was not able to come up with an alibi for when the attack happened. And he offered no resistance about being taken in.

According to the book, *"Perfect Justice"*, by Don Lasseter, Alcala agreed to a taped interview about the 'incidents' from his perspective. He stated that Hoyt had agreed to 'simulate' sex acts with him, and to be tied up as part of the photo session. Alcala admitted that eventually, she began to struggle against the restraints. At that point, he knew her consent stopped. He admitted to choking her until she was unconscious and stuffing her shirt down her throat to stop her from screaming.

When asked next what he had done, his answer was shocking. *"You're in an unreasoning situation. Your brain and you just don't know what to do. You're not reasoning. You're not thinking. I raped her."*

Although prosecutors asked for $500,000 bail, the judge set the bail at just $10,000. Alcala had no problem getting that amount of money from his mother, so he was set free on March 16. The judge set a trial date for September and he walked out of jail, yet again. If this judge had not allowed him bail, his next victims would still be alive.

Chapter 16: Jill Parenteau

Jill Parenteau was only twenty-one years old when she moved into her own apartment in Burbank, California. Like Alcala's other victims, Jill was exquisite in her appearance, and smart as well. She was proud that she could afford her own apartment and when assigned a ground floor initially, she asked for a second floor instead out of concern for her safety.

On June 13, 1979, Jill told her sister she had a date to go see a Dodgers game that evening with a crush from high school. Jill went on the date and came home happy. She was happy that she had a good time with her date and happy the Dodgers won.

The next morning, Jill's best friend, Kathy Bowman, was a bit concerned that she didn't hear from Jill. Part of their best friend routine was talking on the phone every morning, no matter what. Bowman tried to call Jill once she was at work, but again didn't get an answer. She had an uneasy feeling about this. She called Jill's boss, who told her Jill had not shown up for work. Bowman couldn't stand the anxious feeling any longer, so she called a co-worker of Jill's to ask if she would go to her house and check on her. Upon arrival, the co-worker discovered Jill, dead inside her apartment. She became hysterical and called authorities.

When the Burbank Police arrived on the scene, they found a window with a cut screen, and several glass panes removed. They didn't notice any signs of struggle as they walked into the apartment, and nothing seemed out of place. At the back of the apartment, they went into a room and found Jill... on the floor next to the bed, facing up, and nude. Her legs were spread wide, facing the entrance to the room. Her shoulders and back were propped up.

There was serious damage to her teeth, nose, cheeks, and head. Dark ligature marks surrounded her neck. A pair of torn and knotted pantyhose lay on the floor next to her. Clothing and bedding were strewn about the room, covered in blood. The cord of a lamp ran under her body at the neck area. An electric blanket cord also was under her body and wrapped around her neck.

The coroner noted the following damage to Jill Parenteau's body:

"Extensive scalp hemorrhage six inches from side to side, with trauma so severe that she bled into the under surface of her scalp.

Significant pulling or striking blunt traumas to the head by an object broader than a hammer, or the head slammed against a flatter object, or a human fist used against head.

Knots tied in nylons that created ligature marks on neck; severe hemorrhaging through the thyroid, voice box and epiglottis. The victim had been strangled so severely that the small blood vessels in her eyes had ruptured.

Bruises to the tip of the tongue; bleeding inside mouth and injuries to the corner of the mouth, consistent with forcible oral copulation.

Deep scratches around both breasts; tooth marks and puncture type wounds around right breast; puncture wounds below the left nipple and cuts to the left side of the left breast.

Deep wounds to the vaginal and rectal areas.

The coroner concluded that most of the injuries occurred while Jill was still alive.

Cause of Death – Strangulation

Sperm was found inside the oral cavity and semen was observed on vaginal smears.

Inconclusive findings on the anal smear."

In the days after Jill Parenteau's body was found, there was a barrage of attacks on young people in the Los Angeles area. On June 17, a ten-year-old girl named Robyn Billingsly was kidnapped on her way to the beach. She was found the next day, in a ravine, beaten, raped, but still alive. The bodies of two young boys were found in remote areas, and they had been sexually assaulted as well.

Several young girls told police that a man claiming to be a photographer approached them on the beach between June 27 and June 30. The photographer fit the description of Rodney Alcala. They had conversations with him about photos, and a few were even photographed. But they never went to another location with him. It also helped that they were in pairs when they were approached.

On the same day Robin went missing, two other girls in the same area were approached by a man with a camera. The man looked like Alcala. One of the girls posed for him. But her friend wisely insisted they leave, and fortunately for them, they did.

Chapter 17: Robin Samsoe

On June 20, 1979, best friends, Robin Samsoe and Bridget Wilvert, decided to go to Huntington Beach. Robin had a ballet class later that afternoon, but she and Bridget could enjoy the beach before she had to go.

The girls were enjoying summer vacation, hanging out at Bridget's house for lunch, and laying out in the sun until about 1:00. It was only a two-block walk to the beach from Bridget's house. The girls arrived at the beach and found a comfortable spot to chat, laugh, and talk about things that twelve-year-old girls like to talk about.

At one point, they looked up to see a man walking towards them. They giggled at first because he didn't seem dressed for the beach. He wore slacks, and a plaid shirt. They saw a large camera hanging around his neck, and he asked if he could take their picture. He told them they were real pretty, and he needed to take their picture for a photography class. They thought it was funny, but agreed to let him take their photos.

Down the beach, Jackye Young, was watching the scene with interest. She wondered why a grown man, who looked very out-of-place to her because of the way he was dressed, would be taking photos of little girls. When she saw the man reaching to touch one of the girls on her knee, she decided that she would confront the man, just to be safe. When Young got closer to the girls, she realized one of the girls was her neighbor, Bridget Wilvert. She came up behind Alcala, as he was kneeling on the ground between her and the girls. He jumped when she asked what the girls were doing. Instead of turning around to speak to Young, he turned around and immediately walked away. Again, that seemed very suspicious to Young, and she told the girls they should probably not talk to any more strangers. She offered to walk the girls back to Bridget's house.

They had lost track of time and now Robin was afraid she might be late for her ballet class. Robin was excited because this was going to be her first day answering phones for the studio. She was growing up and taking on more responsibilities. She asked Bridget if she could borrow her bike to get back to her house, change for class, and then ride it to the dance studio. Of course, her best friend said yes. The "Stepping Stones Ballet School" in Seacliff Village was only a fifteen-minute bike ride from her house. She would make it in time!

But Robin did not show up for dance class and everyone went into panic mode. There was a flurry of activity from Robin's family trying to contact friends and neighbors. By 1:00 a.m., Robin was declared a missing person by Huntington Beach Police Department.

Over the next few days, a lot of girls from the beach came forward to give information about the mysterious, and oddly dressed, photographer on the beach that day. They described Rodney Alcala, and when shown photos of him, identified him easily.

Robin's broken and abused body was discovered in a dirt gully on July 2, 1979. Because of the length of time between her death and being identified, there was advanced decomposition. Her small body was not intact, and cause of death could not be ascertained.

Chapter 18: Other Victims

"I used to be so in control, but reality is losing its hold
Now I don't know where to begin, just look at the state that
I'm in
My mind is in total decay, I'm coming to take you away"
– "This Maniac's In Love With You" by Alice Cooper

Throughout my research for this book, I spoke with nine women who claimed Alcala attacked them. Out of those nine women, only two ended up in the stories included here. There was a third story, but the woman was far too damaged from what had happened to her, so she declined to give an account of her harrowing experience. Neither of the women who did tell me about their experiences with Rodney Alcala would provide a last name.

I also received a lot of bizarre and unreliable messages from women positive Alcala had attacked them when they were younger. Although I can't say for certain if someone was or wasn't assaulted by Alcala, I can tell when someone is telling me a far-fetched story. Several women who contacted me said they were sure he had raped them, but as it turned out, the attacks were during times he was incarcerated. Unfortunately, these women were wrong about Alcala being their attacker. There are far too many sick men going around brutally attacking women.

One woman told me the oddest story about her encounter with him. She was a relative of one of the most famous true crime authors, and I was surprised at her story. She claimed she had gone with Alcala to his apartment, and when they got there, she had a bad feeling. She asked to use his bathroom, and when she walked down the hallway, she opened the wrong door. Inside that room, she claimed to see several women tied to the walls, with an air-conditioning unit running, making the room "feel like a freezer." She said that some of the women were moaning, and some looked dead. While I suppose it is possible this happened, it sounded more like a scary movie to me.

After meeting a lady by the name of Karen through a social media group in 2013, she told me her story:

"It was sometime in the Fall of 1977 that I was raped and beaten by Rodney Alcala. I think it was October because I remember in the days afterwards there were Halloween decorations out on the house in my neighborhood and in the stores. Halloween has been more than just a scary holiday to me since that day and I never have been able to shake it.

I was a student at San Francisco State University and I was in my second year. I had just turned 20 and thought that everything was safe in the world. I had a normal, happy childhood. I grew up in Oakland California and from the time I was old enough to remember, my parents always said they wanted me to be a doctor, dentist or lawyer. I was smart and got all A-s in High School, but my real dream was to be a model or actress. I had always admired Twiggy, but when Lauren Hutten became famous, I was determined that I could be a model because Lauren had the imperfection of a space between her teeth, like I did. I never smiled because of it until she was famous and I saw her.

I was intrigued the day I saw a man taking pictures of models at a little spot near Fisherman's Wharf. I thought he must have been very famous himself and wondered if he had even taken pictures of Lauren Hutten since he was so handsome. I was with a girlfriend and she wasn't as interested as I was and needed to be somewhere, so I stayed behind to watch him take pictures. I was secretly hoping that he would see me and started to dream that this was the day I would be discovered. I kind of made myself obvious to him and he smiled at me. He eventually came over to me and we talked about my wanting to be a model. He said he was a fashion photographer and had published pictures in Vogue and a few other magazines. He told me I would be a star and that he would help me.

I was completely trusting then and never even thought of the danger there could be in getting into a car with a stranger and driving to a secluded area. He said that it would be a lot better pictures in a nature setting rather than downtown. The only second guess I had was the way I was dressed. I only had jeans and a light sweater on and didn't think this would be good for fashion. But he told me that this actually wouldn't be the actual shoot. He said that this was just a practice photo shoot and he would be able to study how I posed and if it looked good afterwards, he would put me in an evening gown and we would go back and try to recreate it. That seemed to be a good explanation and, what did I know about how these kinds of shoots were done. Plus, I just wanted to be famous, so any pang I had about going there with him went away.

I can't recall what kind of car he had, or the color even. But I do remember it smelled bad and was really dirty inside. We went to San Bruno Mountain Park. He continued to tell me how much of a star I was going to be as we hiked back into an area that he led us to. I didn't notice anything different about him or sense anything wrong. I have read how people sometimes have what they call a gut feeling about something that was going to happen. But I never had that.

He stopped at a spot and pointed down to some trees and said that looked like the best spot. I followed him down and I even remember him helping me with his hand one time when I tripped.

We walked into the trees just a short ways and he started to give me directions on how to pose. I had never done this before, so I was nervous and awkward at first. He cracked jokes and made me laugh. This seemed to go on for quite a while and I became more at ease. He kept looking around though and I asked him what he was looking at. I can't recall the answer, but, again, it seemed reasonable at the time. In looking back on it, I guess I was flirting with him in a way because I wanted to impress him. I was only 20 so flirting was something I thought was fun and harmless. After awhile he suggested that it might be cool if I took my top off and posed in just my bra and jeans. I did it and he kept telling me almost with every pose that I was a natural.

The reason I have told so few people in my life about this is because of my embarrassment at what I did next. I always felt it was my fault because he asked me to take my sweater off and I did. I had taken my clothes off for only 2 men in my life before and, obviously, never for a stranger. The thought of that even today makes me want to cry with shame. I wasn't an angel, and wasn't a virgin, but I sure was far from a loose girl. I don't know what made me do it, but I did. To make matters worse, I wasn't even embarrassed. In fact, I felt more free (sic) being bare on top. As he took my pictures, he asked me to do things like throw my head back and cup my breasts. At his direction, I licked my lips and even pinched my nipples. He asked me to put my hand down my jeans as I leaned forward to him. His attitude changed once I was naked on top and he became breathless and talked faster. He kept looking around, but I just thought he was trying to make sure no one could see me naked. I even unzipped my jeans as he asked and pulled them down a little bit on my hips.

The last posing request I remember him asking me to do was to walk a little bit further into a treed area, turn around, and pull my jeans down just a bit to expose just a little of my bottom, and stick my bottom out.

The next thing I remember was waking up on the ground and my head was throbbing. I was on my back and he was between my legs and above me. He was pulling the last leg of my jeans off. For some reason, I remember the feeling of that last pant leg coming off. I didn't even recognize him because his face was so contorted. I thought I was dreaming. I didn't know where I was. I woke up maybe twice after that and one time I was on my stomach and my body was in just awful pain. Another time I woke up and couldn't breathe. His hands were around my throat and squeezing. The last time I woke up, I hurt so much that I could barely move. I was thinking clearer, but still fuzzy. I was in such terror though that I was frozen. I don't know how long I was in that position, but I heard nothing but the wind. I tried to move a couple of times but hurt so much that I stopped myself. Eventually I was able to turn over and as I looked around, I saw that I was alone. My head was still pounding and I felt dried blood on my face and in my hair. My long hair was caked with blood. It was not dark yet, but I could tell it had been a couple of hours since we'd first gone there. There was a lot of blood around me and on me. I found my clothes and put them back on. I was in shock and every sound that I heard made me jump in fear that he was still there, waiting to finish me off.

I dressed and went back out into the clearing below the path we'd come. I had to sit down a couple of times and threw up three times when I walked out of the area and back to where the parking was. I don't know what I looked like but must have looked pretty bad when I approached a couple of older men who were standing by a car.

There was a family further down, but these were the only people there. I only chose the men to walk up to since they were closest. I had already decided to never tell anyone about this. The two guys there had a shocked look on their face as I almost collapsed into one of their arms. I told them that I had fallen off of a ravine and needed a ride home. Looking back, I see this as another decision that could have turned out wrong. But, at the time, I was barely thinking, let alone thinking correctly. They took me directly home but begged me to go to the hospital. I told them that I was fine, just a bit of a headache and was confused. They couldn't see the injuries under my clothing, but I could barely stand the pain in the lower half of my body.

When I got home, I removed my clothes and examined my injuries. I had been beaten badly. My inner thighs and my knees were black by now with bruising. I was torn in my vagina and I had never had anal sex before, but I could tell from feeling that area that I had been forced by him that way.

The pain from the water was so bad that I almost passed out.

I went to bed afterwards and pretty much stayed there for the next week. I told my friends that I'd been in a car accident and they bought that excuse for why I was moving so slowly. They brought me a few things I needed, but I was terrified at night and would always try to get someone to stay with me. I had healed enough after about a week to go back to classes. But, I was so traumatized going back and forth, and even walking between classes, that I quit after only a few days.

My body slowly recovered, but I guess my mind never did. Looking back, I was pretty lucky not to have gotten an infection or even able to have kids. I never went to see a doctor and only used aspirin and pot to get by.

I don't recall if I heard before or afterwards, but there was a 19-year-old (sic) student at my school who had been murdered on my campus a few weeks before this happened to me. Her name was Jenny Chang and they never found the person that killed her. I read about it more after this happened to me and I really think that it was Alcala who killed her. They found her raped and dead in a room in the library. Supposedly it was a locked room on another floor that no one was using and they said that it had to be someone who worked there because it was locked and no one had a key.

My life has been a good one since then and I married and had my own family. I had problems with drugs and alcohol and always blamed this incident in my life. But I don't really know. I quit the drugs when I was pregnant with my first son and never touched anything like that again. But the alcohol came back over and over through my life. I would quit when I was pregnant and try to stay sober, but it seemed to be impossible. I kept it under control though and had a good job for not having a college degree. My marriage was still good and my kids grew up in spite of the fact that I was a paranoid and protective mother. While I tried to force this experience to the back of my mind, it always surfaced when one of the kids came home late or when they wanted to go somewhere that I was not comfortable with. I was happy that I never had told my parents because it would have killed them. I didn't understand this until I had my own.

Our family had moved away from California in 1990 and I stopped drinking alcohol and haven't had a drink since then. I had a few difficult days, but none so difficult as the day in 2012 when I saw his photo online related to some cold cases in California. It scared me to death because it was like looking at him face to face again. I did a Google search and came across the Facebook page about finding photos that he had taken of other women. My photo was not in that group and I wondered what had happened to the pictures he took of me that day. It took me a while before I contacted the maker of the Facebook page, but I finally got up the nerve and told her my story."

The next story was sent to me by a woman named Lisa. Her story is written verbatim.

"Hi Toria,

Ok, here we go. I will start at the beginning. I moved from Long Island to San Francisco California when I was 17. I moved with a friend of mine named Ginger who had some friends in California. Mike was going to let us stay with him until we found a place of our own. We moved to Golden Gates Heights and it was the beginning of December 1978 I don't recall the exact date.

On December 31, 1978 it was New Year's Eve and the closing of Winterland and the Grateful Dead were playing. We were at a party in the city and as you can imagine New Year's Eve/Grateful Dead. the city was crazy. I barley knew anyone besides my friend and a few of her friends that she knew before we moved there and people were coming in and out of the apartment everyone was drinking and what not.

So here I am a 17 year old girl, drinking, feeling out of place as I was the youngest. This very attractive man came in to the party, so me I am assuming he knows the couple who live in the apartment. So we were talking and being a 17 year old girl I was flattered he was even interested but he was suprisingly charming. He introduced himself as Rod.

In conversation I told him my love for horses. So he said he had a friend who had horses and all we needed to do was groom them and we could ride all day. So once again being a 17 year old I said SURE. he had a trusting way about him. So I told Ginger I would see her the next day.

He said we were going to Half Moon Bay. So we started hitching. I had no idea where we were but I didnt really care it was fun. So we got a ride on Highway 1 Pacific Coast Highway and the person that picked us up pretty much drove us the whole way.

It was dark but there was a house and we walked in and it was a very nice home. Neat as a pin. But Rod said that we were not staying there. We walked out the door and there was a small barn. There were chickens ,but no horses. At that moment I was a little nervous but also a little drunk so I just followed. We went in the barn and there was a ladder going up to a loft, He told me to go up the ladder and I did. He then pushed something against the door it was some sort of motor and I definitely knew then that this was not good.

Up in the loft was a big round foam mattress, but the thing that freaked me out was that there was womans clothes/coats/and pocketbooks. I can still remember seeing girls IDs on the floor so this was not the first time he was here with a girl.

He asked me to take off my clothes, I resisted and he then ripped my pants off me ripping the zipper. I begged him not to rape me but his intentions were to masturbate on me, I was in my underware the whole time and he did masturbate on me as if he wanted me to feel like a piece of shit, a nothing. After that he got on top of me and gave me hickeys all around my neck and on my breast. I just kept my cool as I was always told if ever in this type of situation.

It started raining, I heard the rain on the roof as it was a metal roof. I asked if he would let me down so I could go to the bathroom he said no, He told me to open the window and there was the metal roof that I had to climb out on and pee.

I came back in and he was calm, just talking and wanted me to lie down with him and I did. I had no way out. He was a different person after the masturbation and all that kinda like his job was done.

We laid on the foam mattress and he went to sleep. When it got light out I started looking for my clothes. He woke up and moved the engine from the door and as I was getting dressed he said he owed me a pair of pants, I was like its ok, dont worry about it. And I just went don the ladder and started walking.

There were no horses, just chickens, there were no people, But I turned around and he was watching me walk away. I was just holding my pants up and thinking where the fuck am I. Thank God I have a really good sence of direction and remember when getting out of the car the house was on the left so I walked right. It was a dirt road and the scenery was beautiful. I just kept thinking how can this happen in such a beautiful place. I walked for a long time but I could see the ocean so I knew the highway was in that direction.

I came to a street sign, Verde Dr. I walked to a gas station went to the rest room looked in the mirror and alls I saw was those hickeys. I washed my face and walked to the highway and started hitching. A man picked me up and asked me where I lived and I said San Fransisco and he asked if I was ok? I said yes. Whoever that man was he was my angel. He drove me right to my doorstep. And it was far. No words were spoken I just wish I would have said to take me to the police. But alls I kept thinking is they are gonna look at me a stupid 17 year old from NY that whatever I got I probably deserved.

When I got home I called my Mom and was on a plane with in a few days. Everyone at that time I told my story to kinda rolled their eyes like I was crazy, So I stopped talking about it. It bothered me for a long time still does.

Then thanks to Facebook I found a friend I went to Jr High with and we became friends again. She was NYPD, I told her my story because Rodney was in the news. She was like holy shit you need to talk to someone about this, Being she was NYPD she found out who the cold case detective was. He came to my house and he no doubt knew it was him.

He then got me in touch with a detective in Half Moon Bay and I gave him detailed description of the house the barn how long I walked and Verde Dr. He found nothing. But this was so many years after the fact that things change, There are lots of mountains there. It is very rural.

The NY detective called me not to long after we met and he wanted me to know they found a body in that area, a girl missing from the 1970's. I know something is at that house. I saw it. All the clothes and IDs, I was just lucky, I got away.

I will go back to Half Moon Bay one day. It feels like it was yesterday,

Look forward to hearing from you soon Lisa"

Chapter 19: The Unsolved Murder of Jenny Chang

On September 11, 1977, Jenny Low Chang, was a 19-year-old student attending San Francisco State University. It was a Sunday evening when she left her on-campus dorm room to walk the short distance to the library, for a study group meeting. The library was open until 11 p.m., but Jenny never returned. Her roommate reported her missing the following morning.

A psychology professor found her nude body in a locked room on the fourth floor of the library. She had been brutally attacked, her head savagely beaten, stabbed multiple times, and raped. Jenny Chang had fought her attacker fiercely, and there was a lot of broken furniture scattered around the room.

There were several suspects in her homicide, including a security guard and a faculty member. These rumors arose because the door to the room where she was found was supposed to be locked at 5:00 p.m., and a coded key/card was needed to open the door. Only staff and faculty were allowed with coded key cards. It's possible the room was left unlocked accidentally, or the perpetrator could have opened it ahead of time in preparation for taking a woman there.

The information on this homicide was scarce, however, I discovered that the Zodiac Killer was one of the prime suspects in Jenny Chang's case. Even today, many people still believe he was responsible. Personally, I don't agree with this theory for a few reasons:

- The Zodiac Killer stopped killing in 1969, eight years before the slaying of Jenny Chang. Zodiac committed his first documented murder on December 20, 1968, and his last on October 11, 1969

- Zodiac communicated extensively with newspaper agencies after his murder spree ended, but the final letter attributed to him was postmarked January 29, 1974, and sent to "The Chronicle" in San Francisco, which was years before Jenny Chang was murdered

- Zodiac claimed to have killed 37, however, there were only seven victims proven, and two of whom survived.

- The way Jenny Chang was killed doesn't fit with Zodiac's M.O. All of his victims were shot, with the exception of two. He also didn't rape his victims, and Chang was brutally raped before she was killed.

- It was highly possible that Zodiac was a convenient suspect to name when this case couldn't be solved back then.

Instead of Zodiac, I'm of the opinion that Rodney Alcala was responsible for Jenny Low Chang's murder for the following reasons:

- Not only was her homicide during Alcala's prime killing spree, but it was also the month before Karen, who attended the same college, and was attacked by Alcala. The timing is too much of a coincidence

- Chang was beaten severely about the head, which was in line with Alcala's modus operandi

- Alcala sexually assaulted all of his victims, and Chang was raped.

Sadly, Jenny Low Chang's murder became a cold case decades ago and was never solved.

Epilogue

Alcala was arrested one month after the murder of Robin Samsoe. He was tried and convicted of her murder in 1980, and sentenced to death. However, the California Supreme Court overturned the verdict because jurors had been informed of his prior sex crimes.

This trial was only for the murder of Robin, and it would be years before his DNA would tie him to the murders of Jill Barcomb, Georgia Wixted, Charlotte Lamb, Jill Parenteau, Christine Thornton, Cornelia Crilley, and Ellen Hover.

In 1986, after his second trial, omitting sex crimes, he was convicted again, and again sentenced to death. A Ninth Circuit Court of Appeals panel rescinded the second conviction, however. Partly because Alcala had represented himself in that trial, and there was some information about a witness in that trial that was misleading, and thus should not have been allowed to testify.

In 2006, DNA proved conclusively he had also killed Barcomb, Wixted, Lamb and Parenteau. These four victims were added to the victim list, which already included Samsoe.

At his third trial in March of 2010, the jurors took just one hour to find Alcala guilty of the murders of the four women and one child, after a six-week long trial.

In his final California trial, representing himself, he played a piece of Arlo Guthrie's song "Alice's Restaurant" in which the narrator tried to avoid being drafted for the Vietnam War by trying to convince a psychiatrist that he was unfit for the military because of his supposed intense aspiration to kill.

In January 2013, Alcala was extradited to New York, where he was sentenced to additional prison time for the murders of Cornelia Crilley (1971) and Ellen Hover (1977). The judge handed down a sentence of 25 years to life in prison for these murders, but he would not serve there until and unless he was ever freed in California.

Unfortunately, two other victims would never see justice. Christine Thornton and Pamela Lambson. Alcala would not stand trial for their murders because of his failing health.

****

No one knows when Rodney Alcala decided being a photographer would give him a reason to get close to beautiful women and girls. His attack on Tali Shapiro occurred in 1968, and when he escaped his apartment after attacking her, there was a lot of photo equipment, and photographs of young girls discovered inside.

The concept of enticing beautiful young women with a promise of fame and fortune, was not a new one, and in fact, had been used many times in history. It is just as old as offering candy to a child, or asking for help finding a puppy, or pretending to be injured and needing help.

Alcala probably did have a genuine interest in photography. Who knows. But there is no doubt that his deviant mind found it a safe and seemingly innocent way to get close to young women. What was his intention in the beginning? Did he have murder on his mind and used his photography to lure women? Or did the photography come first, and once he stood before beautiful women, the urge to rape and sodomize became too much for him? Some of the women he photographed walked away free from harm. Were there some women he was able to merely document their beauty with his lens, and not have murderous thoughts? Why some and not others?

When Alcala was arrested in 1979, police discovered a trove of evidence from his crimes inside a storage locker in Seattle, Washington. Not only were there earrings of at least two of the victims, but there were also hundreds of photos of people that Alcala had photographed over the years. The images included a variety of what a professional photographer would have...smiling family photos, and happy individuals doing everyday activities, and some people just grinning into the camera. Many of the photos revealed no more than a street photography session or random pictures in a club.

A few showed young people sitting together in a study group or meeting, enjoying each other's company, smoking a cigarette and laughing together.

A collection like that would not have meant anything to the investigation, had it not been for the hundreds of photos of young women in sexually explicit situations. In March 2010, there were 215 photos released by Huntington Beach Police once all of Alcala's trials and appeals were complete. Most of the photos were of women and girls, but among them were two of young boys. One was naked. This gallery of images has become quite an odd stockpile of potential documentation of multiple, possible murders.

When the photographs became public, they caused a flurry of attention by crime enthusiasts, missing person forums, and cold case agencies from all over the United States. The public finally got to see Alcala's photo collection after the legal process was finally complete, and the murder conviction was upheld. The intention behind the release of the photos was to identify some or all the people in the photo collection. Once the gallery of photos was released, it was on the Internet, on television, and in magazines. A few women came forward to say that they had been photographed by Alcala and were still alive and well. We read some of their stories in magazines or heard them on TV, reliving the long-ago memories of posing for Alcala. They all felt fortunate to be alive.

Even after the women stopped coming forward, there were still a handful of disturbing images that remained unidentified. The ones remaining compelled the viewer to wonder about the picture they were looking at…if that photo was in fact the last photo of that person alive. Some were haunting and very unsettling images.

The photos caused a renewed hope in solving cold cases. Law Enforcement of Huntington Beach received hundreds of calls after the initial release of the photos in 2010. Many from other law enforcement officials seeking information about the possibility that Alcala could be responsible for a cold-case homicide in their jurisdiction. Because Alcala was a cross-country traveler, he could have murdered women in any state in America. Some calls were even international. Two girls in the photos were identified and marked alive after being photographed by Alcala in Denmark years ago.

All of the photos preceded July 24, 1979.

There were also lots of calls from desperate family members, begging for more information on Alcala, and where he was living and when. Many of their daughters had left the house one day, and never returned. Could Rodney Alcala have been responsible for the disappearance of their loved ones?

Rodney Alcala has been on death row at San Quentin, California since 1980. He will never be free. However, it is still within hope that more victims will be discovered through this book. According to authorities, they are still searching for the identities of up to 100 females, and at least two young men from the photos. Since these photos were taken during the years that Alcala was active (September 1968 to July 1979), it is crucial to get this information out to as many people as possible. Decades have now passed. Parents have died. Siblings are getting older. They need closure. They deserve closure.

Appendix A: Alcala's Timeline

August 23, 1943: Rodney James Alcala was born in San Antonio, TX

1960: Graduated from Montebello High School in TX

1961-1964: In the US Army (1961: enlisted, June 19, 1961: entered a program in North Carolina to become a paratrooper, 1963: had an AWOL episode, Early 1964: discharged from the army with diagnosis of a mental disorder, went to live with his mother in California)

Early 1964 - 1968: Lived in California. Attended UCLA

1968: Graduated UCLA with Bachelor of Arts degree

September 25, 1968: Kidnapped, raped, and attempted to murder Tali Shapiro, age 8, at his apartment in Hollywood. Escaped and fled to New York

September 1968: Accepted to New York University's School of the Arts undergraduate program under the alias, John Berger

July 1969: Hired as a drama and arts counselor at a girls summer camp in George Mills, New Hampshire under the alias John Burger

1970 -1971: Worked during the summer as arts and drama counselor at summer camp in George Mills, New Hampshire

June 1971: Graduated from NYU and began working as a photographer, primarily focusing on young women, in Manhattan under the alias John Berger

June 24, 1971: Murdered Cornelia Crilley, age 23, in her apartment in the Yorkville area of Manhattan, New York

1971: FBI placed Rodney Alcala on the Ten Most Wanted List

August 1971: Two campers from the art camp recognized their counselor, John Burger, on the FBI's Ten Most Wanted List while at a local post office. They reported this to their camp director, who confirmed the man listed as Rodney Alcala was his employee, John Burger. He called the FBI. Alcala is arrested for the assault of Tali Shapiro and extradited to California

August 1971 – May 1972: For the crime of child molestation on Tali Shapiro, Alcala received an indeterminate sentencing, which allowed the judge to set a range of time instead of a specific time frame to be served. He received one to ten years, with parole as an option.

August 3, 1974: A state prison psychiatrist determined Alcala to be considerably improved during his term of incarceration. He was released on parole in Los Angeles, CA, under the stipulation that he register as a sex offender with the Monterey Park, CA, police department

August – September 1974: Hired by a photography company to take photos in stores throughout Los Angeles, CA

October 1974: Kidnapped Julie J., age 13, in Huntington Beach, CA, forcing her to smoke marijuana with him before being arrested by a park ranger who smelled the marijuana and decided to investigate

October 26, 1974: Served sentence for charges against Julie J. at the Southern California Reception Center for new California Department of Corrections inmates and parole violators in Chino, CA, and at California's Men's Colony in San Luis Obispo, CA

June 1977: Released on parole. Parole officer allowed Alcala to travel to New York to visit relatives

July 1977: Murdered Ellen Jane Hover, age 23. Her body is not found and she is reported missing. She was last seen with Alcala, who was under the assumed name, John Berger, in New York City, NY. Also, during this month, he visited Chicago and Washington D.C. He was a person of interest in the murder of Antoinette Whittaker, 13, but never tried for the murder.

August 1977: Known to be in El Paso, TX

September 1977: Returned to Los Angeles and hired as a typesetter at the Los Angeles Times

October 9, 1977: Suspect in the murder of Pamela Jean Lambson, age 19, whose body was dumped on a Marin County hiking trail. Although there are no fingerprints or DNA, investigators are convinced that Alcala is responsible.

November 10, 1977: Murdered Jill Barcomb, age 18, in Los Angeles, CA

December 14, 1977: Questioned by FBI in Los Angeles regarding Ellen Hover

December 16, 1977: Murdered Georgia Wixted, age 27, in her Malibu, CA home

February 1978: Suspect in the murder of Joyce Gaunt, age 17, in Seattle, WA

March 1978: Spent a brief amount of time (unknown exact dates) in jail when marijuana was found in his home while being interviewed by the Hillside Strangler Task Force due to his classification as a sex offender.

June 1978: Murdered Charlotte Lamb, age 32. Her body was not identified until September 1978 because he had murdered her in a laundry room of an apartment complex near her home. Lamb had been listed as missing.

June 1978: Remains of Ellen Hover were found in North Tarrytown in Westchester County, New York, after the NYPD Missing Person Squad interviewed people who knew Alcala and determined he was known to take women to that area to photograph them.

Summer 1978: Alcala was "Bachelor number one" on The Dating Game. The show aired September 13, 1978.

September 1978: Charlotte Lamb was identified

February 1979: Raped and assaulted Monique Hoyt, age 15, in a secluded area after she had ben picked up hitchhiking. She gained his trust and escaped from him. He was arrested, but released on $10,000 bail by a Riverside judge,.

April 1979: Alcala gave his two weeks notice at Los Angeles Times

June 14, 1979: Murdered Jill Parenteau, age 21. She was found in her apartment in Burbank, CA.

June 20, 1979: Abducted Robin Samsoe, age 12, while riding her bicycle to dance class. She had met him earlier in the day when he asked to take pictures of her and a young friend. She goes missing for 12 days.

July 2, 1979: Robin's remains are found in a wooded area.

July 11, 1979: Alcala rents a storage locker in Seattle, WA, for photos, photographic equipment, motorcycle, etc. He returned to Los Angeles three days later.

July 14, 1979: Arrested in Monterey Park, and incarcerated pending trial for Robin Samsoe. The receipt for the storage locker was found in his mother's house. He was never free beyond this date.

July 26, 1979: Law enforcement obtained a warrant for the storage locker rented by Alcala in Seattle, WA, and flew there to search the unit. After a three-hour search, police collected several pieces of evidence, including over 1,700 photos and negatives in boxes. They also found jewelry belonging to some of his victims.

Appendix B: The Doe Network

IDENTIFIED....IDENTIFIED.... IDENTIFIED

Unidentified Female

Date of Discovery: April 6, 1982

Location of Discovery: Sweetwater County, Wyoming

Estimated Date of Death: 1980

State of Remains: Near complete or   complete skeleton

Cause of Death: Unknown

Physical Description

Listed information is approximate

Estimated Age: 25-39 yrs old

Race: White

Gender: Female

Height: 5'8"

Weight: 130 lbs.

Hair Color: Brown

Eye Color: Unknown

Distinguishing Marks/Features: Many well healed fractures and 6 months pregnant at time of death.

Dentals: Available

Fingerprints: Not Available

DNA: Available

Clothing & Personal Items

Clothing: Pullover type blouse extensive stitching on the front; Denim type pants with elastic waist band, 2 button closures in the front; clothing is fragmentary and partially torn; Left thick soled shoe and two buckles

Jewelry: Gold Timex wrist watch with a black face and nylon woven band; 2 rings #1 Black hills Gold with Grape leaf design 10K size 6 or 7. #2 Silver wedding or friendship type ring with a Laurel design size 6 or 7.

Additional Personal Items: None

Case History

The body was located in isolated area in Sweetwater County, Wyoming.

She was identified in 2015 as Christine Ruth Thornton. Her sister was looking at the unidentified photos of Rodney Alcala and saw her sister in one of the photos. Christine looked happy and was seated on a motorcycle, wearing a bright yellow shirt and blue jeans. When she was found, she was still wearing the clothing in the photo. She was six months pregnant."

Appendix C: Do You Recognize Any of These Photos?

UNIDENTIFIED 1 | UNIDENTIFIED 1

UNIDENTIFIED 3 | UNIDENTIFIED 4

UNIDENTIFIED 5 | UNIDENTIFIED 6

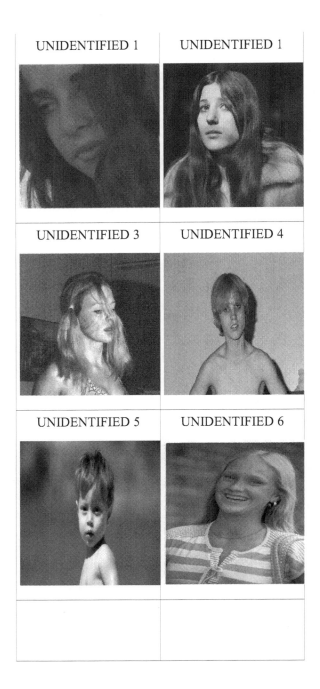

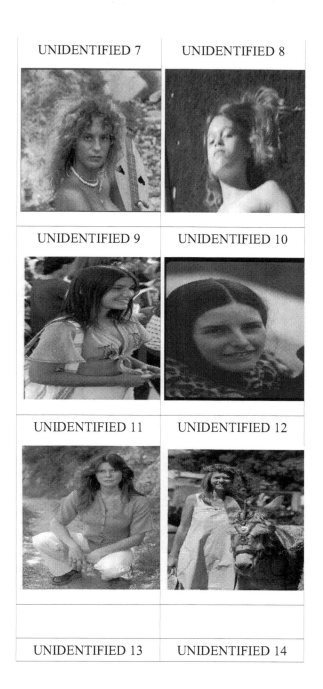

UNIDENTIFIED 7   UNIDENTIFIED 8

UNIDENTIFIED 9   UNIDENTIFIED 10

UNIDENTIFIED 11   UNIDENTIFIED 12

UNIDENTIFIED 13   UNIDENTIFIED 14

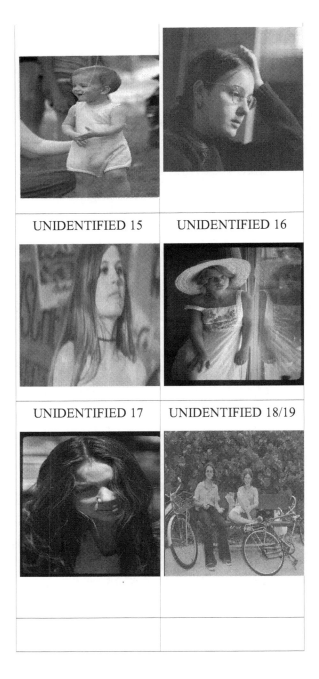

UNIDENTIFIED 15   UNIDENTIFIED 16

UNIDENTIFIED 17   UNIDENTIFIED 18/19

UNIDENTIFIED 20   UNIDENTIFIED 21

UNIDENTIFIED 22   UNIDENTIFIED 23

UNIDENTIFIED 24   UNIDENTIFIED 25

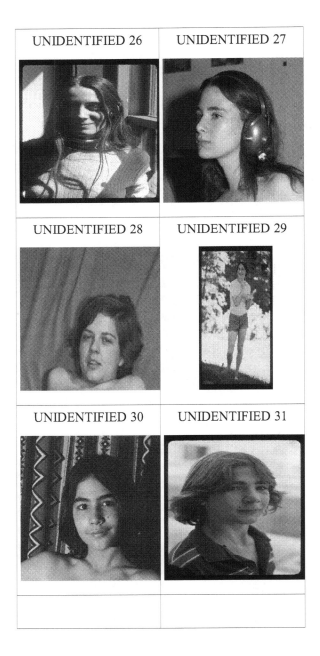

UNIDENTIFIED 26   UNIDENTIFIED 27

UNIDENTIFIED 28   UNIDENTIFIED 29

UNIDENTIFIED 30   UNIDENTIFIED 31

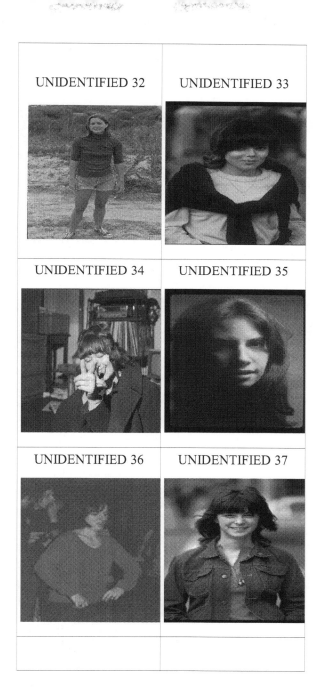

UNIDENTIFIED 32

UNIDENTIFIED 33

UNIDENTIFIED 34

UNIDENTIFIED 35

UNIDENTIFIED 36

UNIDENTIFIED 37

UNIDENTIFIED 38 UNIDENTIFIED 39

UNIDENTIFIED 40 UNIDENTIFIED 41

UNIDENTIFIED 42 UNIDENTIFIED 43

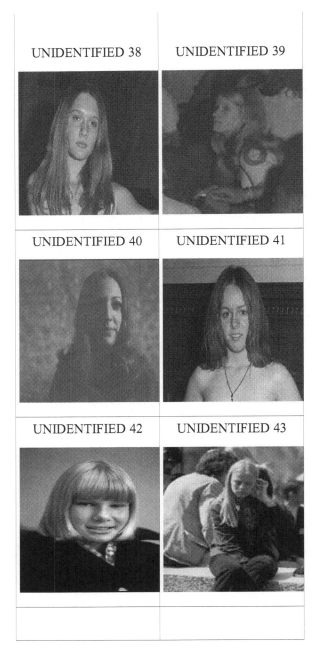

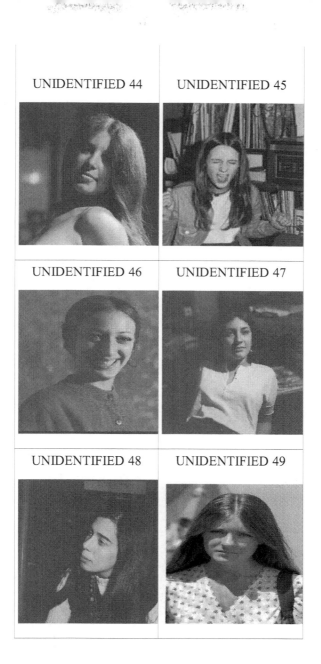

UNIDENTIFIED 44　　UNIDENTIFIED 45

UNIDENTIFIED 46　　UNIDENTIFIED 47

UNIDENTIFIED 48　　UNIDENTIFIED 49

UNIDENTIFIED 50	UNIDENTIFIED 51
UNIDENTIFIED 52	UNIDENTIFIED 53
UNIDENTIFIED 54	

About the Author

As a former 911 dispatcher and private investigator, Victoria has a technical perspective on crime and a passion for victim advocacy. With her first book, *More Than Just a Pretty Face*, she hopes to bring attention to victims instead of predators.

Before she started writing true crime, she gained experience in law enforcement and investigations. She now focuses her time writing about issues that help people better understand how people are impacted by crime.

Victoria is a mother of five daughters, living in a small town in Missouri with her husband, Todd, and two hysterical cats.

You can follow her on Facebook at the group More Than Just a Pretty Face or Twitter twitter.com/crimeresearchvb

References

Rodney Alcala "Dating Game Killer" Information researched and summarized by Ashley Africa, Ariel Bobrick, and Samantha Hough Department of Psychology Radford University Radford, VA 24142-6946

Diana Dimond - Volume 1 – Serial Killers

https://www.sweetwaternow.com/dating-game-killer-will-not-extradited/

Autopsy report of Jill Barcomb, Georgia Wixted, Jill Parenteau – Stella Sands (The Dating Game Killer)

Letter to anonymous fan by Rodney Alcala

Dating Game Killer by Stella Sands

Information researched and summarized by Ashley Africa, Ariel Bobrick, and Samantha Hough Department of Psychology Radford University Radford, VA 24142-6946

Serial Killers Encyclopedia by RJ Parker, 340p, May 2014

Made in the USA
Middletown, DE
24 August 2019